CICERONIANL

OR

A Dialogue on the Best Style of Speaking

BY

DESIDERIUS ERASMUS

OF ROTTERDAM

Translated by IZORA SCOTT, M. A.

With an Introduction by PAUL MONROE, Ph. D.

Published by
TEACHERS COLLEGE, COLUMBIA UNIVERSITY
NEW YORK CITY
1908

PRESS OF
BRANDOW PRINTING CO.,
ALBANY, N. Y.

Editor's Introduction

A few words concerning the setting and the educational significance of this treatise are desirable by way of introduction. The *Dialogus Ciceronianus* (1528) is the one important technical educational treatise of Erasmus, that has never appeared in an English form. Even in the original, it has had few reprints and none of these are of recent date. His *De Ratione Studii*, and the treatise *De Pueris Statim ac Liberaliter Instituendis* are given in English by Professor Woodward in his *Erasmus Concerning Education;*[1] the *Colloquies* have appeared in several forms, most completely in the Bailey edition;[2] his letters, which contain much discussion of direct educational value, are adequately represented in the recent Nichols edition;[3] but the *Dialogus Ciceronianus,* his most extensive treatise on an educational subject as it demanded attention in his own day, has not been deemed of sufficient interest to the student of education to justify a translation.

In the broad significance of the term, almost all of the works of Erasmus are educational. As Professor Saintsbury remarks,[4] "Very great man of letters as he was, and almost wholly literary as were his interests, those interests were suspiciously directed towards the applied rather than the pure aspects of literature— were, in short, *per se* scientific rather than literary proper." This suspicious practical interest constitutes the characteristic which gives his writings educational value. His dominant interest in scholarly work was to remove ignorance of literature and of life in the past, and to furnish a proper basis for the study of these by the editing of numerous classical texts; to establish proper standards of life's value and of conduct through his satirical and controversial writings; and to furnish a proper basis for formal educational processes through adequate linguistic aids. In following out the first of these motives he issued his critical editions

[1] Cambridge University Press, 1904.
[2] *The Colloquies of Erasmus.* NATHAN BAILEY, 1733, with various later issues.
[3] *The Epistles of Erasmus from His Earliest Letters to His Fifty-first Year.* Translated by F. M. NICHOLS, London, Vol. 1, 1901; Vol. 1904.
[4] SAINTSBURY. *History of Literary Criticism,* Vol. 3, p. 10.

of Terence, Seneca, Cicero, Suetonius, Plautus, etc., and above all, his editions of the various church Fathers, notably Jerome. His critical editions of the New Testament, both in Greek and in Latin, had the same general design. In his efforts to remove the ignorance and improve the moral customs of his generation, he wrote the *Colloquies, The Adages,* and the *Praise of Folly.* But satire, while an efficient weapon for the destruction of moral evils, of prejudices founded on ignorance, of provincialism and of bigotry, is not an adequate or even a safe instrument in the education of youth. While Erasmus gave comparatively little attention to the problems of the school-room or of private instruction, yet many of his colloquies and letters relate to this field of activity; the *Adages* as well as selections from the *Colloquies* served as texts, and he gave some assistance in the preparation of grammatical and rhetorical aids to this end.

The interest of the student of education is necessarily focused on this latter phase of the subject,—namely, on the problems of instruction, such as the choice of material, the methods of teaching and of study, the organization of schools or of the instruction process, the forms of discipline and of control and the immediate aims and purposes of instruction and of school work. These and similar technical problems are considered in the treatise *De Ratione Studii* and *De Pueris Statim ac Liberaliter Instituendis,* in various uses of the *Colloquies* and *Letters,* in his *De Conscribendis Epistolis* and in a portion of the *Christiani Matrimonii Institutio.* All these educational discussions are concerned with the problems of the new humanistic education as opposed to the traditional education of the schools under ecclesiastical influence. Even where the traditional conception of the middle school—the Latin grammar school—was modified and the classical materials of study accepted, the spirit of the school, the methods of control, and methods of study, the treatment of pupil by teacher and of teacher by society remained much the same and needed to be reformed. The elaboration of suitable methods of linguistic and literary study was the work of some generations and, though much had already been done, Erasmus also contributed much.

Professor Woodward's scholarly discussion[6] of these and similar topics leaves little to be desired by the student of the history

---

[6]WOODWARD. *Erasmus Concerning Education;* Cambridge University Press, 1904.

of education who must draw his introductory knowledge of the subject through an English source.. With this discussion available, any elaborate treatment of Erasmus' ideas concerning education and school work is unnecessary at this time. But the other aspect of Erasmus' work, his conflict against the obscurantists of his own school of thought, has not been sufficiently emphasized; nor is the material available to our students for the consideration of this phase of the educational situation of the period when the humanistic ideals were being reduced to schoolroom procedure.

New ideas and standards once established, remained long in vogue. In fact the education of the 15th and 16th centuries erected much of the structure that the pedagogue continued to inhabit until well into the 19th century. Slight additions were made to enlarge the structure, but a structure upon an entirely new design awaited the 19th century. Now it is because the above-mentioned educational writings of Erasmus dealt with this structure that stood so long,—and dealt with it in the making,—that a general interest in them has been preserved, that they have been put into English and that they have been treated by the technical student of education.

But the nature of the *Dialogue on Ciceronianism* is wholly different and it appeals to a different interest, as it also illustrates another phase of education during the 15th and 16th centuries. Erasmus waged a two-fold battle in the interest of rational educational ideas and practices; one against the obscurantists of the traditional type, the scholastic and orthodox ecclesiastical educators. The other was against the extremists of his own party. The conception of education held by these latter was no less narrow and little less repulsive than the old, their method of school work was little less efficient and under them the school was no less inadequate to the performance of its proper social function than was the case under the traditional usages. This bitter conflict, however, was of an ephemeral character. In time any system of school practices tends to degenerate into formalism and to lose vital contact with the underlying principles, but the danger to a broad reformatory system from the extremists among its own devotees is not apt to be a vital one during the period of its establishment, nor is the discussion around the quantitative interpretation of such principles apt to be of such permanent value as the qualitative discussions bringing those principles into relief against those absolutely contradictory.

Knowledge of such a discussion may be essential to an understanding of the educational situation at that time but not of much practical and immediate value to the practitioner under the system when once established. For this reason the *Dialogue on Ciceronianism* has received little attention; and for the reason that it throws bright light upon the educational situation in the time of Erasmus, it deserves study.

The importance of the mastery of linguistic form had been so exaggerated by many of the humanistic educators that Cicero had come to exercise an authority in the new schooling that in many instances was no less tyrannous, no less harmful and no less misrepresentative of the educational principles presumably involved than did Aristotle in the old. Many humanists had come to look upon Cicero as the exclusive model for all Latin composition. Though their influence was not yet so dominant that they could control the schools, it was powerful enough to affect and profoundly influence the views of many of the lesser humanists and so of many school men. Such Ciceronians would use only the words and constructions found in the writings of their master and would use any circumlocution to accomplish this end. The effect upon the schools and the humanistic world in general was especially pernicious in two respects: there was an elimination of Christian authors from the course of study and a distinct disparagement of Greek. To Erasmus, style was subordinate to the ends to be accomplished; to the Ciceronian, style was the ultimate goal. To such men much of Erasmus' writing was crude if not barbarous. Many, no doubt, did surpass him in polish or perfection of style, but none in effectiveness in accomplishing the common aims of the humanists,—the removal of ignorance and prejudice and the freeing of individual judgment from the trammels of arbitrary authority. That some able classical scholars should seek to impose a new type of authority aroused his scorn, even though that authority should be a humanistic one,—Cicero himself. Such views represented to Erasmus an utter perversion of the humanistic spirit.

But an objection to this servile and pedantic imitation of Cicero that was of greater weight to Erasmus than the linguistic, literary and educational one was the moral and religious effect of such misplaced devotion. The extreme classicists were forced to avoid the discussion of Christian theories or to employ in such discussions titles and terms borrowed from pagan mythology and pagan civilization. Thus some Italians were guilty of using the term Jupiter Maximus for God the Father, Apollo for Jesus Christ, *divi* for saints. Cardinal Bembo had treated pagan themes as frankly as the ancients themselves. He warned Sadoleto to beware lest his style be corrupted by reading the *Epistles* of St. Paul. Against such an exaggeration of the value of the classics Erasmus even defends the language of the Thomasts and Scotists, in that their style at least conformed to their subject-matter. The entire passage in the dialogue devoted to the discussion of the effect of extreme devotion to classicism on religion is of peculiar interest. Erasmus argues that were Cicero now living and a Christian, he would use Christian terms, quote from the scriptures as he does from earlier Latin authors, and that he would follow as the fundamental principle of style, the fitting of style to the thought. He urges further that this undue evaluation of Ciceronian style is a large factor in perverting our taste and our understanding; that many come to take more pride in being a Ciceronian than in being a Christian. This was but one aspect of a minor phenomenon peculiar to the renaissance, the reversion to paganism. Erasmus did not hesitate to call it so.

Even if this aberration was not quite so extreme as it became in Italy, the free discussion of religious questions was greatly hampered by a strict adherence to the language of the purists. While Erasmus was interested in improving the vulgar Latin, and replacing the scholastic terminology with a more classical form, he was even more interested in improving the manners and morals of his times by a clearer understanding of Christian principles and doctrines as well as by a knowledge of the best of customs of the ancient classical world. Among these possessions of the Roman civilization to be coveted and striven for were universal peace, toleration of religious practice, freedom of individual opinion in religious beliefs and other matters of opinion, a universal language, a free interchange of opinion throughout the whole of Europe, the cultivation of literary taste and ability through a broad choice of authors of both Greek and Latin literature, and the fostering of schools for general social ends. Now the extreme classical view furthered the attainment of none

of these ; on the contrary it produced discord, limited the freedc
of the individual, failed to use the classical literature as an educ
tional means for the development of personality, stifled individ
ality, made the work of the school mechanical, and above all e
tirely overlooked the influence of Christianity as the chief fact
in the solution of the grave social problems, and neglected t
great need for a better understanding of biblical and patris
writings as a basis for religious and moral reform.

The *Dialogue*, however, grew immediately out of a person
situation, as did most of the controversial writings of Erasm
and of his contemporaries, however broad the significance a
influence of the discussion. Erasmus had been the obje
of many bitter attacks on the part of various Italian a
French humanists. Actuated in part no doubt by jealousy of l
great reputation, envious that an uncouth German or at least
barbarous Northerner should have so great public acclaim, sor
of these attacked him in the most vulnerable place,—the sen
tiveness of a scholar for his reputation for scholarship. In the
days, when scholarship frequently formed a sufficient motive f
a most laborious life and when its rewards in public esteem we
second to no other, such an attack was most apt to be felt a
most apt to be resented.

Erasmus had successfully withstood the various charges
heresy,—at least had avoided conviction of heresy though co
stantly persecuted by the monks. It is true that the *Colloqu*
had appeared comparatively recently (1519), and had arous
widespread and bitter opposition within the church. The bo
was condemned by the Sorbonne, prohibited in France, and
fact was interdicted by the papacy to all Christendom. Desp
the opposition, the second edition (1522) sold over 26,000 copi
and more than seventy-three editions appeared during the autho
lifetime with more than 200 editions since. While this wo
became a weapon of tremendous power in the destruction of t
abuses of the old church, it did not escape the opposition of t
reformers, especially of Luther, for it was in fact a dangero
means of education of the youth.

But recently Erasmus had sufficiently alienated the Luthera
by his treatise *On the Freedom of the Will* (1624), so that
could not now be attacked on the religious side with as dir
results. This *de Libero Arbitrio* had been called forth by Lut

er's extreme emphasis on the Augustinian doctrine of salvation through God's grace, the total unworthiness of man and his utter inability to keep God's law, in favor of the church's long established doctrines, though not necessarily of its practices, concerning the efficacy of works. The work drew a heated reply from Luther (*Hyperaspistes*, 1526). Despite the efforts of Melanchthon and other mutual friends, the outcome of the controversy was that Erasmus, who had once been Luther's " dearest brother " and " most honored of men " became "that venomous viper Erasmus of Rotterdam, the most inflated soul in all the world." Erasmus, in somewhat more temperate phrase, accused Luther of ignorance, impudence, blasphemy and even untruthfulness. His final judgment was that ultimately Luther would be held in greater execration than any other man, while Luther spoke of Erasmus " as the worst enemy that Christ has had for a thousand years."

When the conflict began a former colleague or school-fellow was on the papal throne as Adrian VI (1521-23) and Erasmus hoped for much from him, both in the way of personal favor and of successful dealing with the bitter religious controversy. Ever a lover of peace and a hater of strife, Erasmus recommended a liberal treatment of the " heretics," the abandonment of persecution and retaliation, and a reunion on the basis of a reform in morals. But the pope demanded, as an evidence of good faith, that Erasmus should use his influence and his pen. The mild-mannered beginnings of an attempt to conciliate shortly led to vituperative controversy, and his early interest in the efforts of the reformers was entirely lost. For a long time Erasmus had been growing out of sympathy with their aims as he always had been with the Lutheran manner if not the Lutheran methods. His sympathy with the humanistic aspirations of the papacy were of long standing. Erasmus' association with the earlier Medichean representative on the papal throne, Leo X (1513-21) had been friendly and enjoyable, though all that he had hoped from such an enlightened rule of the church did not eventuate. Previous to this time, during his visit to Italy (1506-1509) the Italians and especially the churchmen had shown him great honor. Bologna had given him a degree; at Venice he had lived with Aldo; and everywhere the powerful churchmen, now the patrons

.of learning, showed him great honor. ¡Prominent churchm⋅
tried to induce him to make Rome his permanent abode.

His sympathies were now definitely with the old church a⋅
there remained. Erasmus was now an old man,—he was ju⋅
under three score years at the beginning of his personal contr⋅
versy with Luther and was sixty-two when he wrote the *Cicer⋅
nianus*. His departure the following year from Basel where ⋅
had for so long found his happiest residence, but now ma⋅
untenable to him because of the progress of protestantism a⋅
the consequent violent destruction of much which he held valuab⋅
if not sacred, is but another evidence of the revulsion of ⋅
feeling against the protestants. Freiburg, where he now took ⋅
his residence, was an episcopal stronghold of orthodoxy and ⋅
that time within the Austrian dominion. The next six years, t⋅
last few but one of his life, were spent in peace and for the mo⋅
part in the preparation of religious works, of a devotional rath⋅
than of a controversial character.

But it is the literary controversy which centered arou⋅
the *Dialogus Ciceronianus* with which we are concerned, thoug⋅
the occasion for that controversy is partially explained by ⋅
recent religious writings and the ecclesiastical situation. F⋅
it is from those whom he might expect to be more friendly b⋅
cause of religious and intellectual sympathies, that much of th⋅
criticism came.

Much of this criticism of lack of scholarship came from Ita⋅
where the two papal secretaries Bembo (1470-1547) and Sad⋅
leto (1477-1547) were the leading humanists and the former, ⋅
least, the representative of the extreme Ciceronian views.¡ Itali⋅
opponents were now unable to make capital of their ecclesiastic⋅
position to bring Erasmus into disrepute through religious pers⋅
cution, and in truth Sadoleto was little less liberal than Erasm⋅
or at least was temperamentally similar. In critical scholarshi⋅
the two Italians mentioned and other humanists also, notably t⋅
Frenchman Budaeus, stood higher in the estimation of his ow⋅
and of subsequent times. Naturally such men resented the pop⋅
lar acclaim given to Erasmus, his much greater success as ⋅
writer and the much greater influence of his scholarship. Whi⋅
these men were not the authors of the scurrilous charges, Era⋅
mus considered them indirectly responsible for some of the⋅
as he complained to Sadoleto that they were permitted to emana⋅

from Rome. Among other things he was charged with stealing some of his translations; his emendations were said to be guesses; his annotations a series of blunders. His name was written Er-rasmus to indicate the frequent errors which he made.

Erasmus had no good grounds for complaint that his enemies should use the same controversial weapons which he did so effectively and so constantly; though satire is no argument and ridicule is but a poor weapon of defense. With the very general alienation of protestant sympathies, it seems odd that Erasmus should deliberately stir up the opposition of those influential at Rome just at the time that he might expect the favor of their sympathetic influence. But the fundamental ground of the criticism was the same in both cases. Throughout his life Erasmus had been consistent in this one thing: he had rejected favors, patronage and positions,—ecclesiastical, scholastic and political,—which would limit the freedom of personal action, the opportunity of devotion to study and to literary work, or of expression of opinion. It is often suggested that his attack on Luther in the defense of the freedom of the will was a characteristic act of timidity on Erasmus' part; that, urged by his friends at the papal court to attack Luther he did so on a technical scholastic and theological point of such subordinate interest that it would arouse little interest, though it would be a public repudiation of the reformation leader, now that it was evident that reconciliation was no longer possible. But the point chosen for attack was exactly the one where Erasmus would differ fundamentally from Luther. It was this tendency of the reformer to elaborate a new theology, and to change the basis of disagreement from a moral and practical one to a scholastic and theoretic one that alienated so many of the humanists, as later it was the elaboration of the Calvinistic theology that drove so many of the French humanists back to the Catholic fold. It was this same tendency to erect a new authority and to limit the freedom of individual opinion so hardly won, that definitely determined Erasmus to part company with his Lutheran co-workers. Precisely the same general views now prompted him to take up combat against those who threatened the hardly-won freedom of personal development and expression in the educational, intellectual and literary aspects of life. Even in his old age he dared enter the double conflict.

It is not clearly demonstrated that the *Ciceronianus* was directed towards any particular individual. It has been thought by many that Bembo, the former papal secretary, was the original of Nosoponus. But if so, his correspondence with Erasmus does not show it, as the interchanged letters are friendly after this date as they were before. The *Dialogue* itself mentions Longolius as the only north European worthy of the title. It was undoubtedly the general pedantic tendency of the extremists as well as personal criticism extending over many years together with some particular experiences such as those cited in the *Dialogue* itself that occasioned its publication.

Later Julius Caesar Scaliger (1484-1538) and Etienne Dolet (1509-1546), French scholars, entered the arena against Erasmus, chiefly on the grounds of his fancied slight to Guglielmus Budaeus—the most noted of French classical scholars. As Froude remarks about the attacks on Erasmus inspired by the Lutheran controversy over the "Freedom of the Will," so again in this controversy "the mud volcanoes of the day burst into furious eruption."

The *Dialogue* was Erasmus' one great contribution to literary criticism[6] and his pedagogical confession of faith, though given in no didactic form. There are two main tenets in the faith of the Ciceronians as set forth in the *Dialogue*, neither of which Erasmus will allow. The first of these was that there was an absolute standard in the use of language, and that this perfection of style was attained by Cicero. This belief was the product of the later Renaissance when grammatical study had made considerable progress and numerous treatises on style had appeared and were widely read. The most comprehensive objection which Erasmus, and numerous humanists who agreed with him, had against this was that it made of Latin a " dead " language, and not one to be used as a medium of communication covering all intellectual affairs. It was this latter view which had been held by all the earlier humanists. The earlier humanistic schools had sought to develop such a command of the language by their pupils. But such a conception was threatened by these extreme admirers of Cicero. Erasmus argues that with such a use language becomes extremely artificial and not a means to the expression of thought; that there was no one model of style; further that Cicero does not cover all of Roman culture, that all of his writings are not extant and that there are definite defects in the style itself. This last if not the former views was considered sacrilegious by extreme partisans, and called forth vituperative criticism.

The second tenet of the Ciceronians was that, having demonstrated Cicero to have the master style, a proper style of writing Latin in any age and for any purpose was to be formed by direct imitation of the master. As all possible varieties of styles had been used by the ancients and all were inferior to Cicero, there was no call for and no justification of individuality in style. They further argued that eclecticism in style lacked all unity—in fact, was not style—so that the student or writer was left but one choice,—that of selecting the most nearly perfect stylist and following him as closely as possible.

These views call forth Erasmus' most biting satire and ridicule. *Nosoponus,* the Ciceronian of the *Dialogue,* boasts that he has read no other author than Cicero for seven years, that he may eliminate from his own vocabulary every un-Ciceronian phrase. He has compiled a huge lexicon of every word used by Cicero; another one of Ciceronian phrases; another of paragraph introductions and endings; another of words used in various senses by Cicero. Not only is his selection of words determined by the Ciceronian usage, he eschews the use of particular forms of the word not found in Cicero. Writing is a most laborious task. Six nights must be given to compose a letter of as many sentences, then it is revised ten times and then laid aside for future examination. This, though only a note requesting the return of a borrowed book. No matter if it is too late, providing only it is Ciceronian. When *Bulephorus* objects that such delay is impossible, the characteristic Erasmian reduction to an absurdity occurs in the Ciceronian's reply that he avoids all conversation as far as possible, and when forced to speak would use the vernacular, or would confine himself to his stock of Ciceronian phrases carefully memorized for all ordinary occasions.

The entire dialogue is in characteristic Erasmian vein. The opening scene is a farcical dialogue on the new disease—Ciceronianism—with incidental ridicule of some other professional humbugs of the day. Such also is the banter which follows in regard to the family life. The true Ciceronian can not have his attention divided by the cares of a family or the interruptions of a wife or children. In fact composition can be carried on only in a special room on the interior of the house, " with thick walls, double doors and windows, and all the cracks stopped carefully with pitch and plaster so that by day scarcely a ray of light can break through or a sound unless it is unusually loud such as that of women's quarrels or of workmen's hammers." Not even a house fly may be permitted in to disturb his attention. But under the banter throughout lies the serious argument; while the latter half of the dialogue is devoted to an estimate of the style of the leading classicists, from the time of Cicero to his own day. In this there is fair praise of those rivals for public esteem of his own generation who might consider themselves most offended by Erasmus' strictures, though in fact much of the subsequent criticism of Erasmus was caused by omission as well as by the offence of positive criticism. For especially the friends of Budaeus, himself a friend and correspondent of Erasmus for many years, considered that his claims to distinction were not sufficiently recognized.

But there is no need for an analysis of the dialogue to be given here. Several such already exist with which the interested student is familiar. What the student needs is a careful perusal of the entire treatise. Indeed from an analysis one obtains but a very poor conception of the forcefulness of the discussion, for its power consists not so much in the argument as in the entire atmosphere which it creates which one must breathe to catch the inspiration of the Erasmian ideas and controversial spirit, as well as to feel the stupefying influence of the Ciceronians. It scarcely needs to be mentioned that the entire delineation of the Ciceronians is a satirical one and is not to be interpreted as an historical presentation or a scientific analysis. Yet it is just because the *Dialogue* pulsates with life that it possesses its literary charm and its educational significance.   P. M.

Translator's Preface

The translation follows the text of the Lugduni Batavorum,
edition (1703) of Erasmus' complete works. The aim has been
to render into English the literal Latin as far as possible, depart-
ing from it only when the main object of expressing the argument presented in the dialogue was better subserved by omission
or freedom. Errors, no doubt, have occurred because of failure
to trace out in every instance allusions and references. The
erudition of Erasmus taxes too heavily the ordinary encyclo-
paedias and dictionaries. Acknowledgment is most gratefully
rendered to Professor Nelson G. McCrea, of Columbia University, for assistance and kindly advice in the translation.

I. S.

2

Ciceronianus

OR

A Dialogue on the Best Style of Speaking

Bulephorus: Whom do I see walking yonder in the most re-tired part of the porch? If I am not mistaken it is my old friend and fellow student, Nosoponus.

Hypologus: Is this that Nosoponus who was once the most charming of all jolly companions, delightfully ruddy and stout, bubbling over with Loves and Graces?

Bu.—The very one.

Hyp.—Whence this new shape? More like to ghost he seems than man. Has he some disease?

Bu.—Yes, a very serious one.

Hyp.—What I pray? Not dropsy?

Bu.—The ailment is deeper than the skin.

Hyp.—It isn't that new kind of leprosy which people to-day flatter by the name of mange?

Bu.—The infection is indeed deeper than that.

Hyp.—It isn't the spitting malady?

Bu.—The trouble is more deeply seated than in the lungs.

Hyp.—It isn't jaundice?

Bu.—It is something deeper than the liver.

Hyp.—Perhaps a fever ravaging the veins and heart?

Bu.—It is a fever, and yet not a fever, something burning deeper, advancing from the inmost recesses of the mind. But cease vainly divining. It is a new kind of disease.

Hyp.—Has it then not yet a name?

Bu.—Among the Romans, not yet. The Greeks call it Zelo-duléan.

Hyp.—Has it come on recently? Or is it a trouble χρόνιον.[1]

Bu.—For more than seven years the unfortunate man has been suffering. But we are observed. He seems to be turning his

---

[1] Of long standing.

steps hither. You will find out better from him what the trouble is. I shall act the part of Davus; do you help the conversation along and take a part in the play.

Hyp.—Indeed I would do it gladly, if I knew what you desired.

Bu.—I desire very much to relieve my dear old friend of so serious a malady.

Hyp.—What. Are you skilled in medicine?

Bu.—You know that there is a kind of madness that does not take away the whole mind, but affects one part only in such an extraordinary degree that the victims believe they wear bull's horns on their heads or are burdened with long noses or carry on scrawny necks great earthen heads sure to be broken if they move ever so little, or think themselves dead and shudder at the approach of the living.

Hyp.—Yes, I know.

Bu.—There is no better way to heal them than to pretend that you have the same trouble.

Hyp.—I have heard frequently of that cure.

Bu.—It shall be tried in this case.

Hyp.—Not only a spectator of this play, but a willing helper will I be, for I am particularly well disposed toward the man.

Bu.—Then compose your countenance and play your part so that nothing may suggest to him that there has been an agreement.

Hyp.—It shall be done.

Bu.—I bid Nosoponus a very hearty good-day.

Hyp.—And Hypologus salutes Nosoponus.

Nosoponus: Indeed I wish you both the same in turn. And may your wish for me be realized!

Bu.—It could not fail, if giving were as easy as wishing. But, pray, what is the matter; for your thinness forebodes some ill or other? There is clearly some trouble with your liver.

No.—With my heart, my dear sir.

Hyp.—Heaven forbid! I hope it is not incurable.

Bu.—Is there no help from doctors?

No.—In human remedies there is no hope. Help must come from above.

Bu.—A dreadful disease! But succor from what god, pray, must you have?

No.—It is the goddess who is called by the Greeks, πειθώ·[1]

Bu.—I know, the goddess which moves men's souls.

No.—I am desperately in love with her and am doomed to die unless I win her.

Bu.—No wonder you pine away, Nosoponus. I know what a powerful thing Love is and what it is to be νυμφόληπτον·[2] How long have you been in love?

No.—The years are almost ten since I began to roll this stone with no avail. But I am determined to die in the attempt or gain at length the object of my love.

Bu.—You tell of a love as enduring as it is unhappy, since in so many years it neither has been able to fade nor to win its object.

Hyp.—Perhaps the possession of his nymph pains him more than the lack of her.

No.—On the contrary, I am pining away for want of her.

Bu.—How is it possible? When you alone of all up to the present time have so excelled in eloquence that many say of you what formerly was said of Pericles, "Persuasion sits upon your lips?"

No.—In a word, all eloquence except Ciceronian is distasteful to me. This is that nymph for love of whom I am pining away.

Bu.—Now I know your trouble. You are seeking to gain that splendid and longed for name, Ciceronian.

No.—So much that I consider life bitter unless I attain it.

Bu.—Henceforth I cease to wonder; for you have directed your mind to the attainment of a most beautiful thing; but the common saying is only too true, δύσκολα τὰ καλά.[3] I am in my heart looking with favor upon your wishes myself, if some god will turn propitiously to me.

No.—What do you mean?

Bu.—I will tell you, if you can suffer a rival.

No.—What do you mean?

Bu.—Love of the same nymph distracts me.

No.—What! You possessed with the same desire?

Bu.—Completely, and the flames increase daily.

---

[1] Persuasion.
[2] The captive of a nymph.
[3] "The beautiful is hard to attain."

No.—Indeed in that role you are dearer to me, Bulephorus; for/though I have always esteemed you highly, now also I shall begin to love you, since our minds unite in a common wish.|

Bu.—You would, perhaps, be loath to be cured of this disease if some one should promise help from herbs, gems, or charms.

No.—It would be killing, not curing. Either I must die or attain. There is no middle ground.

Bu.—How easily I divined your mood from my own.

No.—I will hide nothing then from you, initiated, as it were, into the same mysteries.

Bu.—Be assured, you can speak with safety, Nosoponus.

No.—Not only the splendor of a most beautiful name torments me but also the insolent impertinence of those Italians, who, though they approve of no language at all except Ciceronian and think it the greatest disgrace for one not to be a Ciceronian, nevertheless declare that the honor of this name has never fallen to any on this side the Alps except to Christophe de Longueil, recently deceased, of whom (that I may not seem to grude him due praise) I would make bold to declare what Quintilian wrote of Calvus, "Early death did him an injury."

Hyp.—The too early death of De Longueil did less injury to him than to letters. For what could he not have recovered in literature if to such genius and industry the gods had added a fair space of life?

Bu.—But what hinders that which has been given to one, by the consent of the Muses, to belong to others?

No.—He died while engaged in this most noble work, fortunate, I think; for what is more beautiful, more glorious, more magnificent than for a Cisalpine to be called a Ciceronian by the vote of the Italians?

Bu.—I think he is to be congratulated upon his good fortune in dying at the right time, before any shadow darkened his glory either because of growing zeal for Greek letters or a cloud arising from the Christian authors from whom perhaps he would not have kept himself absolutely if he had lived longer.

Hyp.—I agree with you that he was fortunate to die while engaged in this most noble task; but I hope that we shall survive, not perish in our work.

No.—I second your wish! Upon my life, I prefer this honor to being canonized.

Bu.—Who pray would not rather be celebrated in the eyes of posterity as a Ciceronian than as a saint? But since this kind of love knows no jealousy, I beg you in the name of our common hopes and fears to share with me at least your plans—how you seek to win your mistress. Perhaps we shall both gain her more quickly if we help each other.

No.—The Muses know not envy, much less the Graces, companions of the Muses. To the comrade of one's aims nothing must be denied. All possessions of friends should be common.

Bu.—You will make me perfectly happy.

Hyp.—Will you receive me too into your alliance? For I have long been driven by the same frenzy.

No.—We will. Now I shall reveal the mysteries to those consecrated, as it were, to the same god. For seven whole years I have touched nothing except Ciceronian books, refraining from others as religiously as the Carthusians refrain from flesh.

Bu.—Why so?

No.—Lest somewhere some foreign phrase should creep in and, as it were, dull the splendor of Ciceronian speech. Also I have enclosed in their cases and removed from sight all other books lest I should sin inadvertently; and hereafter there is no place in my library for any one except Cicero.

Bu.—How neglectful I have been! Never with such care have I cherished Cicero.

No.—Not only in the chapel and library but also in every doorway have I a picture of him beautifully painted, and I wear one engraved on a gem so that he may ever be in my thoughts. No other vision comes to me in sleep except that of Cicero.

Bu.—I do not wonder.

Hyp.—Among the apostles in my calendar I have given a place to Cicero.

Bu.—Quite right. For they used to call him the god of eloquence.

No.—I have been so diligent too in reading and rereading his writings that I have learned by heart almost all of them.

Bu.—What industry!

No.—Now I am girded for imitation.

Bu.—How much time have you allotted for this?

No.—As much as for the reading.

Bu.—It is too little for such an arduous task. Would that there might fall to my lot, even at the age of seventy, the glory of so illustrious a name!

No.—But hold, I am not content with this. There is not a word in all the books of that divine man which I have not set in order in an alphabetical lexicon.

Bu.—A huge volume it must be.

No.—Two strong carriers well saddled could scarcely carry it on their backs.

Bu.—Whew! I have seen them at Paris who could carry an elephant.

No.—And there is a second volume even bigger than this in which I have arranged alphabetically the phrases peculiar to Cicero.

Bu.—Now, at last, I am ashamed of my laziness.

No.—There is a third.

Bu.—Whew! A third too?

No.—It had to be. In this I have gathered all the metrical feet with which Cicero ever begins or ends his periods and their subdivisions, the rhythms which he uses in between and the cadences which he chooses for each kind of sentence, so that no little point could escape.

Bu.—But how can it be that the first volume is so much greater than the whole of Cicero?

No.—Listen and you will understand. You perhaps think that I am content to note the mere words.

Bu.—I thought so. Is there more?

No.—On the contrary, that is a mere beginning.

Bu.—How?

No.—See how far you miss the mark. The same word is not always used in the same way: for example, the verb *refero* has one force when Cicero says *referre gratiam;* another, when he says *Liberi parentes et forma corporis et moribus referunt;* another, when he says *Refero me ad intermissa studia;* again another, when he says *Si quid erit, quod mea referat scire;* finally another, when he says *Non ignota referam.* Likewise *orare Lentulum* is one thing; *orare causam* is another. Again, *contendit* at one time means *he strives with another;* at another time it means *he earnestly seeks something from some one;* at another time, *he strives with great zeal to accomplish something;* and at another *time, he puts together two things and compares them.*

Hyp.—Wonderful! This is drawing up a veritable λεξικοὺς ἐλέγ-χους.[1]

Bu.—Now, at last, I appreciate both your industry and my laziness.

No.—I do not note individual words unrelated but give the context. And I am not satisfied to have noted one or two passages as some are; but as often as the word is found in Cicero, however similar the form, I note the page, the side of the page, and number of the line, affixing a mark which indicates whether the word is in the middle of the line, at the beginning, or at the end. In this way you see one word takes up several pages.

Bu.—Ye Gods! What may not such care accomplish!

No.—Just a second, Bulephorus. You have heard nothing yet.

Bu.—What else can there be?

No.—What advantage to know a word if you stumble on its forms, derivatives, compounds?

Bu.—I do not know exactly what you mean.

No.—I will explain. What more trite or common than the verbs: *amo, lego, scribo?*

Bu.—No question about these, is there?

No.—Or than these nouns: *amor, lectio, scriptor?*

Bu.—Nothing.

No.—But believe me it is both necessary and needful for one who seeks the dignity of the title, Ciceronian, to be so exact that he will not use these very common words without weighing their meaning—unless, perchance, you think it safe to trust to the Grammarians, who inflect verbs through all moods, persons, genders, and tenses, and nouns, pronouns, and participles through all cases and numbers, though we have no right to use any of them not used by Cicero. It is not great to speak like a Grammarian, but it is divine to speak like Cicero.

Bu.—Explain, I pray, more fully.

No.—*Amo, amas, amat* (for this may be cited as an example), I find in Cicero; but *amamus* and *amatis* perhaps I do not find.

---

[1] Inventory of words.

Likewise I find *amabo*, I do not find *amabatis*. Again *amaveras*
I find, *amaras* I do not; in contrast, *amasti* I find, *amavisti* I do
not. And what if you should find *legeram, legeras, legerat,* and
should not find *legeratis?* If you should find *scripseram* and not
scripseratis? In the same way you may form conclusions about
the inflections of all verbs. About the inflections of the cases,
the method is the same. *Amor, amoris, amorem, amori,* I am
sure of in Cicero; *O amor, hos amores, horum amorum, his amori-*
bus, O amores, I do not find. Likewise *lectio, lectionis, lectioni,*
lectionem, I find; *lectiones, lectionibus, lectionum, has lectiones,*
and *O lectiones,* I do not. So *scriptorem* and *scriptores,* I find;
scriptoribus and *scriptorum* as a substantive noun I do not find.
These things of course must seem ridiculous, if you are bold
enough to use *stultitias* and *stultitiarum, vigilantias* and *vigilanti-*
arum, speciebus and *specierum, fractuum, ornatuum, cultuum,*
vultuum, ambitibus, and *ambituum,* and innumerable others of
this sort. From these few examples you can judge concerning
all which are inflected in the same way.

Hyp.—[1]*Intenui labor.*

Bu.—[2]*At tenuis non gloria.*

No.—I too will join in the refrain,[3] *Si quem numina laeva*
sinunt, auditque vocatus Apollo. Now about derivatives—*lego*
I should dare to use, *legor* I should not; *nasutus* I should,
nasutior and *nasutissimus* never; *ornatus* and *ornatissumus,*
laudatus and *laudatissimus* I use without hesitation, *ornatior* and
laudatior I scruple to use unless I find them. Nor would I
dare to say *scriptorculus* and *lectiuncula* just because I find in
Cicero *scriptor* and *lectio.*

Bu.—I see an immense forest.

No.—Now learn about compounds. *Amo, adamo, redamo* I
may say but not *deamo. Perspicio* I may use but not *dispicio.*
Scribo, describo, subscribo, rescribo, inscribo I may say; *tran-*
scribo I may not unless I have found it in Cicero's works.

Bu.—Do not tire yourself by citing in detail. We understand
perfectly, Nosoponus.

No.—The smallest volume of all contains these.

Bu.—A camel's pack.

---

[1] Vergil G. IV. 6.   Slight is the subject,—
[2] But not slight the praise.
[3] If heaven assist and Apollo hear my lays.

Hyp.—And indeed a full one.

Bu.—How comes it that you make no mistakes in such a wilderness?

No.—In the first place I do not rely upon the Grammarians or other authors however well approved, or precepts, or rules, or analogies, which deceive most people. In the Elenchus I take note of all inflections of root words, derivatives, compounds. Those that occur in Cicero I mark with a red mark; those that do not, with a black. So it is not possible to make a mistake.

Bu.—What if a word is found in Terence or in an equally approved author? Will it be marked with a black mark?

No.—There is no exception. A Ciceronian he will not be in whose books there is found a single little word which he cannot show in the writing of Cicero: and a man's whole vocabulary I deem spurious just like a counterfeit coin if there is in it even a single word which has not the stamp of the Ciceronian die; for to him alone, as the prince of eloquence, it has been given by the gods above to stamp the coin of Roman speech.

Bu.—The law is more severe than those of Draco, if a whole volume is condemned, however choice and eloquent it otherwise is, on account of one little word unlike Cicero's.

Hyp.—But it is fair. Do you not see that on account of one little counterfeit piece of money great wealth is confiscated, and on account of one wart, however small, the whole form of a maiden, otherwise beautiful, is robbed of charm?

Bu.—I grant it.

No.—If now from what I have said you draw a conclusion as to the whole, you will see well enough the bulk of this volume—how much larger it is than the volume in which I have gathered the formulas of speech, tropes, figures, gnomes, epiphonemas, witticisms, and all like sweet morsels of speech; or than the third volume which contains all the rhythms and feet in which Cicero begins, develops, and ends his periods. For there is no passage in all Cicero which I have not reduced to definite feet.

Bu.—This load would surely need an elephant carrier.

Hyp.—You mean a wagon.

No.—But I am not misrepresenting at all.

Bu.—Truly your seven years have not been ill spent. Now that you are finely equipped with dictionaries, tell us, as συμμύσταις·[1] how you are accustomed to turn this noble collection of yours to the needs of speaking and writing.

No.—I shall keep no secrets from you. And I shall speak of writing first, as it has been said truly that the pen is the best teacher of eloquence.

In the first place, I never gird myself to writing, except at dead of night when profound quiet and deep silence reign over all, or if you prefer Vergil's lines:

> [2]Placidum quum carpunt fessa soporem
> Corpora per terras, sylvaeque et saeva quierunt
> Aequora, cum medio volvuntur sidera lapsu,
> Quum tacet omnis ager, pecudes pictaeque volucres.

Or again, when there is such tranquillity that if Pythagoras were alive he could hear clearly the harmony of the celestial spheres. For at such a time the gods and goddesses delight to join in converse with pure souls.

Hyp.—At that time of night the uninitiated are afraid of meeting ghosts.

No.—But the Muses have given us power to scorn ill-omened ghosts and the carping crowd.

Bu.—Yes, but there are nights so quiet that the winds amuse themselves with falling houses and piteous ship-wrecks.

No.—I know, but I choose the perfectly tranquil nights. Ovid has aptly said: [3]*Est deus in nobis, agitante calescimus illo.* If, as I was saying, the soul of man has anything divine it comes out in this most profound silence.

Bu.—I have noticed that the seclusion of which you speak is seized upon by the most able men whenever they attempt anything worthy of immortality.

No.—I have a library in the most inmost part of my house with thick walls, double doors and windows, and all the cracks stopped carefully with pitch and plaster so that by day scarcely a ray of light can break through or a sound unless it is unusually loud such as that of women's quarrels or of workmen's hammers.

---

[1] Friends and brothers.
[2] When wearied bodies through the lands are snatching peaceful sleep: when forest and fierce seas are calm; when in the middle of their course the stars are rolled; when all the earth is silent; silent all the herds and winged things of varied hue. Vergil—Aeneid IV. 522-5.
[3] There is a divinity in us, and when he stirs our souls we glow. Ovid F. 6, 5.

Bu.—Thundering of human voices and noises of workshops certainly prevent concentration.

No.—Not even in an adjoining room do I allow a bed lest talking in sleep or snoring break in upon the privacy of my thought.

Hyp.—Frequently the shrew-mice disturb me at night when I fain would write.

No.—In my house there is not even a fly.

Bu.—You are indeed wise and fortunate as well, Nosoponus, if you can shut out also the anxieties of the mind; for, if they accompany us into our retreat, what shall we have accomplished by our seclusion?

No.—You are right, Bulephorus. I know that those turmoils are often more troublesome than the hammers of neighboring workmen.

Bu.—What about love, hate, envy, hope, fear, jealousy? Do they never trouble you?

No.—To answer briefly, always bear this in mind, Bulephorus, that those who are bound by love, jealousy, ambition, avarice, and like diseases vainly seek this honor for which we are candidates. Such a divine thing requires a heart not only free from all vice but also from all anxiety, just as do those more occult sciences—Magic, Astrology, and Alchemy. Though these lighter cares yield readily to keen and serious attention, yet I drive them away if there are any such, before I enter that sanctuary, for there I have accustomed my mind to close study. I have decided too that it is most important to remain unwed; not because I ignore the sanctity of marriage, but because a wife, children, and relatives can but bring with them much cause for anxiety.

Bu.—You are wise, Nosoponus; for if I should prepare to work on Cicero to that extent at night my wife would burst open the door, would tear the books, and would burn the pages that are absorbed in Cicero. And what is even more intolerable, while I was working on Cicero, she would find another lover.

No.—Since I know that some have had this experience, I have taken warning and have guarded myself in time. For the same reason I have not wished to undertake any public duty or ecclesiastical office, lest some anxiety should come to my mind.

Bu.—Yet these offices are sought by others most eagerly.

No.—Indeed I do not envy them. As for me, better than a consulate or rule of the pope is it to be and to be considered a Ciceronian.

Hy.—He loves truly who can love but one.

No.—In the second place, if I am preparing for anything of this kind I forego dinner, having also breakfasted lightly, lest something of crass matter should invade the seat of etherial mind or lest some cloud exhaled from the stomach should weigh down and [1]*affigat humo divinae particulam aurae.*

Bu.—Thus I believe Hesiod was affected when he wrote.

Hyp.—But [2]*Ennius ipse pater numquam nisi potus ad arma prosiliit dicenda.*

No.—And therefore he wrote songs redolent of wine.

Bu.—And [3]*satur, quum Horatius dicit Ohe.*

No.—We are not concerned with poetic frenzy. To be a Ciceronian is a sober task.

Hyp.—My brain deserts me when I fast.

No.—It is not absolutely fasting. I take ten small raisins, the kind they call currants. This is neither food nor drink and yet it is both.

Bu.—I know. They dissolve slowly and aid the brain and memory.

No.—And three coriander seeds coated with sugar.

Bu.—Excellent. To counteract the currants .

No.—And I do not choose nights indiscriminately for this work.

Bu.—No? You have excepted those on which the winds rage. Possibly you avoid winter nights on account of the cold.

No.—A glowing hearth readily dispels that discomfort.

Hyp.—But sometimes smoke and the crackling of fuel is distracting.

No.—I use wood so dry that it emits no smoke in burning.

Bu.—Well, what nights do you choose?

No.—Favorable seasons for this work are few indeed, therefore I choose auspicious nights.

---

[1] Chain to earth that particle of essence divine.   Horace Sat. 2. 2. 79.
[2] Horace Epistle 1. 19. 8
      Father Ennius ne'er caught up his lyre
        To sing of fights, till wine had lent him fire.—Martin.
[3] He is filled when Horace says Ohe!   Juvenal Sat. VII, 62.

Bu.—By what means, pray?

No.—By astrology.

Bu.—Since you are so completely engrossed in Cicero how have you leisure to learn astrology?

No.—I bought the book of an expert in this art. I act upon his advice.

Hyp.—I hear that many have been deceived by such books, because the author has reckoned wrong.

No.—I did not buy until I had examined it carefully.

Bu.—This is what writing means! Then I no longer marvel, Hypologus, that our works are crude and unpolished. But tell me, according to this rule, which is of first importance, attention to subject or to language.

No.—Both.

Bu.—You have given me a puzzle, not an answer.

No.—But I will explain the puzzle. In general, attention to subject matter is prior to thought of words; in particular, it is secondary.

Bu.—It is not quite clear what you mean.

No.—I will make it clear with an illustration. Imagine that I have decided to write to Titius asking him to see, as soon as possible, that the books are returned which I loaned, if he wishes our friendship to continue, for something has happened that I am in great need of them. If he does this, there is nothing in my possession which he may not consider his own; if not, I shall break the bond of old friendship. Here no doubt the first thought is of the facts, but in a general way.

Bu.—I see.

No.—Then follows the question of the words. I read as many letters of Cicero as possible; I consult all my lists; I select some words strikingly Ciceronian, some tropes, and phrases, and rhythms. Finally, when furnished sufficiently with this kind of material, I examine what figures of speech I can use and where I can use them. Then I return to the question of sentences. For this now is a work of art to find meanings for these verbal embellishments.

Hyp.—Just as an illustrious workman prepares an exquisite dress, necklace, rings, and gems; and afterward fashions a waxen image upon which he may fit these adornments, or rather, which he may mould to the adornments.

Bu.—Why not? But come Nosoponus, is the whole night given to one letter?

No.—Why do you say *one?* I deem myself very fortunate if a winter night shall have finished a single sentence.

Bu.—Do you write such long letters upon so trivial a subject?

No.—Not at all. Very short ones, not more than a half dozen sentences.

Bu.—And it takes six nights to finish it?

No.—As if it were enough to write just once. Ten times must you reshape what you have written, ten times test it by your dictionary lest by chance some little counterfeit word may have escaped you. Then there is still the examination of tropes and phrases and, lastly, of rhythms and style.

Bu.—No wonder it is a task to finish your work.

No.—Not even is this enough, my dear sir; for, since the finished work is your greatest possible anxiety, it must be laid aside for several days so that after an interval, when the love of invention has grown cold, you may cull, as it were, the barbarisms which are your own. Here then a severe censorship is exercised. This is a severe, and, as the Greeks say ἀδέκαζον[1] judgment, when he who writes ceases to be a parent and becomes an Areopagite. Here it often happens that you turn your pen and erase everything.

Bu.—It is true that in this way your books show the result of great care but in the meantime the other type of writer enjoys some books which you have not.

No.—This inconvenience I should prefer to submit to rather than to send forth anything which is not Ciceronian. Each one is led by his own judgment. I prefer quality to quantity.

Bu.—We have your theory of writing. What preparation do you make for speaking?

No.—The first precaution is, not to converse in Latin if I can help it.

Bu.—Not in Latin? Yet they say that by practice we learn to speak well. It is a new plan to learn to speak by keeping silent.

No.—By speaking we come to speak readily but never to speak Ciceronian Latin. Those who prepare themselves for equestrian contest keep the blooded horses from the course

---

[1]Unbribed.

that they may come to race with unimpaired strength. The hunter keeps back the high-bred dog till the game is seen. French or Dutch is good enough for babbling about trifles. In common and profane conversations I do not contaminate the sacred tongue. But, if I am compelled to speak in Latin, I speak briefly and carefully. And for this purpose I have some set phrases.

Bu.—What phrases do you mean?

No.—For example, when you must greet or return the greeting of a learned friend whom you chance to meet; or you must compliment one who has complimented you; or must congratulate one who has returned from a long trip abroad or recovered from a serious illness; or must thank someone who has done you a favor; or congratulate one who has recently married; or condole with one whose wife has died,—for these and like occasions I have provided myself with phrases selected and arranged from Cicero. I have learned them so that I may use them, as it were, *ex tempore.* Then if an occasion arises that the conversation must be extended further, by much reading I wash away the taint. And I am not unaware how great a wrong I am committing through this very conversation which is being held with you, how great a loss I am sustaining in the matter of my ambition. Indeed a month's reading will hardly make amends.

Bu.—Suppose you have time for meditation?

No.—Then I learn carefully what has been worked out in this way; and, in order that I may remember better, I repeat them to myself so that when occasion arises I may pronounce them as if from the written word.

Bu.—What if some exigency should demand an extemporaneous speech?

No.—How can that happen to one who has no public life? But if I should have occasion I am not better than Demosthenes, who would never get up unless he had prepared himself however much he was called by the shouts of the people. And I could not think that I need be ashamed of what is praised in the chief orator among the Greeks or that I should be sorry for the censure if any one should say τὸν λύχνον ἀπόζειν·[1]

---

[1] That my language was bookish.

Bu.—I admire your purpose and your determination more than I can tell. Indeed, I should feel envy if in this kind of enterprise or among such fast friends and companions such misfortune could befall. But inasmuch as what we seek is arduous and the way is not only long and difficult but doubtful, even if the danger were peculiarly your own, nevertheless I should think it due to our long and intimate friendship that I advise my friend unreservedly: lest he undertake so many cares and spend many wakeful hours with loss of health and property to no purpose; lest he continue to do this when once he has begun; and lest, as too frequently we see happen in human affairs, instead of a treasure long and diligently sought he find only charcoal at last. And since we all are led by the same desire and are held by the love of the same nymph (for even Hypologus is of the same mind) it will be an act of kindness on your part to listen to our advice and, if you have anything better, to suggest it freely to your friends.

No.—A very reasonable thing, Bulephorus. Therefore I shall neither listen to you unwillingly nor if I can give any advice shall I make the contribution grudgingly.

Bu.—In the first place this is agreed between us, I think, that he who seeks a reputation for writing or speaking, having learned and mastered carefully the rules of his art, must choose from the many noted writers a master whom he will imitate and whom he will set himself to reproduce.

No.—Yes.

Bu.—But there is no one at least among the Romans who excels in more points of eloquence than Cicero of whom with perfect right it has been said, as was said of Apelles, "In him alone was fused whatever was extraordinary or singular in other painters."

No.—Who can deny this?

Bu.—You will pardon me if I draw my conclusions rather crassly and roughly, for I am unversed in logic.

No.—Anything goes among friends. And yet in general he reasons acutely enough for me who reasons truly.

Bu.—Well, what then do you think of Zeuxis of Heraclea?

No.—What else than what is worthy of the most excellent draughtsman?

Bu.—And this, for you think him to have great talent and wisdom?

No.—How could so great skill be without wisdom?

Bu.—You answer well. What idea then occurred to him when about to paint the picture of Helen for the inhabitants of Crotona —a picture in which he determined to put all the power of his art and to bring forth a perfect and lifelike example of womanly beauty (for in this kind of work he is said to have excelled others) in which no portion of charm would be missing? He did not use as a model the most beautiful woman, but from all who offered themselves to him he chose several who were more excellent than the rest in order that he might select from each what was most comely, and thus at last he completed that wonderful monument of his art.

No.—His work was most carefully done.

Bu.—Consider then whether we are following the right plan when we think we must seek our model of eloquence from Cicero alone, however excellent he may be.

No.—If Zeuxis had found a virgin of such beauty as Cicero, perhaps he would have been content with one single model.

Bu.—Yet in what way could he have reached this very decision, if he had not carefully examined many?

No.—Believe me. I am firm.

Bu.—You think then that there is no virtue worthy of imitation in other orators not found in the highest degree in Cicero?

No.—Yes.

Bu.—And that there is no blemish in him which is not greater in others?

No.—Exactly so.

Bu.—In this connection I will not cite [1]Marcus Brutus, who disagreed entirely with Cicero; for, although the main contention of the defense and the propositions of the division are the pillars, as it were, of the case and the chief part of the argument in *Pro Milone*, which we all so admire, Brutus disapproved of the first and second points employed by Cicero, and handled the same case in a different way. I will not cite [2]Pomponius Atticus, whose finger nails and red pencil Cicero says he feared. I will not cite Cato who called Cicero ridiculous when he thought

---

[1]Quintilian Inst. Or. III. c. 6. & XII. c. 1.
[2]Ep. Ad Atticum XV, 14, & XVI, 11.

himself most witty. Thus far I have mentioned men who are of importance and friends of Cicero. If I add Gallus, Lartius, Licinius, Cestius, Calvus, Asinius, Caelius, Seneca too, and many others, who not only have not felt deeply enough the genius of Cicero but have even condemned his kind of oratory—some calling him dry, jejune, sapless, bloodless, disjointed, weak and unmanly; others, bombastic, Asiatic, and redundant—you will say that these are judgments either of enemies or of jealous persons who, exiled by proscription of the triumvirate, have sought if not to destroy, at least to dull his fame.

No.—You divine rightly. For I certainly should have given this very answer and I think it would have been perfectly fair.

Bu.—Although these judgments may be attributed to hate and envy, you will surely acknowledge that with all scholars wit is a part of the rhetorical art.

No.—If not, why should orators lay so much stress upon it?

Bu.—No one denies that Cicero indulged much in joking. Some say too much, even out of season and almost bordering upon scurrility. Certainly a great majority of scholars hold that in this he lacked moderation just as Demosthenes lacked ability; nor does [1]Quintilian exonerate him when he puts the blame on Tiro, who allowed the number of Cicero's *bon mots* to become far too large and who showed more zeal in collecting than in wisdom in selecting them. In fact, this criticism of Tiro falls back upon his patron. But, however this may be, did any one ever in point of wit give the first rank to Cicero? Wit was the peculiar gift of the Spartans and after them of the natives of Attica. It was so exclusively theirs, that, when the pastoral poem and comedy was most highly praised for its grace and wit, the Romans did not even aspire to it. There is, therefore, some oratorical excellence which is more rightly sought from others than from Cicero.

No.—We are speaking of the Romans.

Bu.—Well, do we dare to compare the jokes of Cicero with those of Caius Caesar or of Octavius Caesar?

No.—Hardly would I dare what no scholar has dared.

Bu.—Well then, if the theme should demand mirth, it would not be right for me to borrow from the wit of Octavius?

No.—Not if you wish to be a Ciceronian.

---

[1]Inst. Orator. VI, c. 3.

Bu.—Again, may I ask whether you class moral reflections among ornaments of speech?

No.—Gems they are and shining lights. Far be it from me to exclude them from art.

Bu.—My next question. Do you think Cicero excelled all others in these reflections?

No.—I know that [1]Seneca ranked Publius [2]Mimographus first in this; but it does not follow that Seneca's estimate is true, for he is extravagant and indulges in certain foibles.

Hy.—You mean to say that the judgment of Quintilian and of Aulus Gellius could be disregarded because they both seemed jealous of Seneca; one on account of rivalry, the other on account of likeness in talent and diction?

Bu.—Yes, but this same Gellius, even granting him unfair, acknowledges that among Seneca's reflections there were some which could not be surpassed,—and one could not expect all to be equally good when the whole work is made up of them. Truly from Seneca's reflections you can find something to imitate more easily than from others where maxims are neither frequent nor striking. But tell me, does a subject sometimes demand brevity?

No.—Perhaps.

Bu.—Will you seek the best example of this from Sallust or Brutus or Cicero?

No.—Cicero has not striven after brevity.

Bu.—In Demosthenes forcefulness is praised, that is, something vigorous and natural. From which of the two shall we seek this most properly?

No.—We are speaking of the Romans.

Bu.—But these are common points of all languages. Again, sometimes the subject demands austerity. Shall we seek this more rightly from Cicero or Brutus and Pollio?

Hyp.—If I may answer for my friend here, from the latter who are distinguished for this characteristic.

Bu.—When the case is involved, when it must be set forth in divisions, shall we go to Cicero or to Hortensius and his school?

---

[1]Epis. VIII & Cap. IX ad Marciam & Cap. XI. de Tranquill.
[2]Writer of mimes.

No.—Why shall we go to one of whom there is nothing left but a memory?

Bu.—But for the sake of the argument let us imagine that his works are extant.

No.—There is no need of imagining. Let us deal with the known and the true.

Bu.—Everyone will acknowledge that trustworthiness in an orator is the chief thing. A reputation for honesty and serious-mindedness gains this, while a suspicion of artfulness and lack of moderation lessens it. While Cicero may be considered a good man—a thing which Fabius, though a strong partisan of his, hardly dares to allow; yet we must admit that he makes a greater display of his skill, boasts more, and inveighs more freely against others than Cato, Brutus, or Caelius to whom Quintilian ascribes conscientiousness. Do we not then more properly seek an example of these things from Aristides, Phocion, Cato, or Brutus than from Cicero?

No.—One would think you had come to this conclusion by studying how to disparage Cicero.

Bu.—By no means. If you will wait the end of my speech, you will see that I am pleading Cicero's case along with our own. For Cicero I am pleading that we may not obscure his glory by imitating him badly as unskilled painters are wont to dishonor those whose portraits they have made quite different from the originals; for ourselves, that we may not misplace our affection and fall upon something as ridiculous and unfortunate as is said to have happened to Ixion who embraced an unsubstantial cloud instead of his beloved Juno, or to Paris who for stolen Helen waged war ten years, all the while embracing a counterfeit image of Helen, while she herself, no doubt, had been carried far away to Egypt by the cunning gods. For what is more unfortunate for us or more ridiculous if nothing results from all our toil except a false and empty shadow of Cicero?

No.—God forbid!

Bu.—Such is my prayer and I am doing all I can to prevent it.

No.—It is helpful in our imitation of Cicero to hold the highest possible opinion of him.

Bu.—It is a new standard of truth, however, if we think of Cicero better than he thinks of himself. Grant that it may be attributed to his modesty if he speak disparagingly of himself.

Yet did any one of the ancients ever so admire Cicero that he thought all ornaments of speech ought to be sought from him alone?

No.—Perhaps not, but today very many think so.

Bu.—I care not at all for your *very many.* I do not believe that any one person is all wise. Has nature yet favored any mortal even in a given field so that he alone excels all others in each particular division; that he has left nothing to be desired; or that he has accomplished so much that he could not be excelled by others? How much more incredible is this in oratory which involves practically all fields of study, which demands many things that cannot be reduced to rules! Let us imagine Cicero alive today and also some such one as 'Trachallus. Would you prefer to seek modulation from Cicero or from Trachallus? I think from the one who was master of all in this particular. Would you prefer to seek a pattern of propriety and modesty from Crassus, if he were alive, or from Cicero? In general, would you not take from each that in which each excelled?

Hyp.—Who, except the indiscriminating or envious, would not choose the better?

Bu.—Therefore the example of Zeuxis commands my approval, and of Quintilian who taught that not just one model must be chosen nor yet all nor any at random but some few choice ones, among whom he gave Cicero first but not sole rank; for he wished him to be foremost among the masters but not alone.

No.—If we give ear to the counsels of Quintilian we shall share his experience.

Bu.—What pray?

No.—That we shall fall short of the Ciceronian standard. We aim higher than that.

Bu.—Will he fail to be Ciceronian who has something more than what he has gotten from Cicero?

No.—So they say.

Bu.—Even if what he gets from someone else is better or is not in Cicero?

No.—Why not?

---

[1] See Quintilian X, 1, 119.

Bu.—In passing I would have you consider, most excellent Nosoponus, what proportion of Cicero's books have perished, among which is that divine work, *De Republica,* a fragment of which by some fate or other preserved torments our souls with a constant desire for the other volumes and allows us to judge the lion, as they say, by the claws—not to mention, for the moment, the many volumes of letters, the many orations stolen by the waste of time, the three volumes in which Cicero's freedman Tiro is said to have gathered his jokes and clever sayings, and the utter loss of his other writings How then can you be a perfect Ciceronian who have not read so many of his works? Add that Cicero has not handled all subjects. If, therefore, we are compelled to speak on themes which he has not touched, where, pray, shall we seek a store of phrases? Shall we go forth into the Elysian fields to ask him in what words he would have described such things?

No.—Those themes only will I handle which can be expressed in the words of Cicero.

Bu.—Well, do you not think that Cicero is the most excellent of orators?

No.—By far.

Bu.—And Apelles? Is he not the best of painters?

No.—People say so and I believe it.

Bu.—Would you call him an Apellean who could paint pictures only from studies which Apelles had painted before, and who also had not seen all the pictures which had been painted by the hand of Apelles?

Hyp.—Who would say this except perchance that painter of Horace's jest, who being hired to paint a shipwreck painted a cypress and asked his patron, who expressed indignation, whether he wished to be painted clinging to the cypress?

Bu.—What else is Ciceronianism except something exactly like this?

No.—It is nothing else.

Bu.—Does he seem like Cicero who can speak only on a limited number of subjects?

No.—Go on.

Bu.—He would be considered in my mind unworthy of the title even of orator. If Cicero was able to speak most excellently upon any subject you please, he to me would be a Ciceronian who could discourse skillfully upon any theme whatever; just as he would be an Apellean who could portray with his brush the forms of gods and men and of living things.

No.—For my part I deem it a greater accomplishment to write three letters in Ciceronian style than a hundred volumes in any other as polished as you please.

Bu.—But if this idea is definitely fixed in our minds, I fear not only we shall not become Ciceronians, but we shall even seem strangers to Cicero. Tell me, I pray, truly, do you think that Cicero must be imitated in every point or in part?

No.—In every point as far as he goes and wholly.

Bu.—How can we imitate him completely when he has not expressed himself completely? Furthermore, how mutilated he is and scarcely half extant in that field in which he has accomplished most! And in the very works which are extant he has not always satisfied himself. For he, as it were, condemned *De Inventione* and substituted *De Oratore*. And he calls the oration in behalf of Dejotarus a poor work. And again, in those books which he merely wrote and did not even revise Cicero himself was not a Ciceronian,—for example, *De Legibus* and many others. How then can we take him for our only example who is mutilated and abridged and sometimes uncorrected and unnatural? Unless perchance you are going to approve of one who, by imitating the unfinished canvasses of Apelles or the rough statues of Lysippus, would hope to become a second Apelles or Lysippus. If Apelles himself, who they say was a man of frank and independent mind, of free and splendid genius, should see this, would he not exclaim, "What are you doing Κακόζηλε·[1] This is not Apelles." If one had before him as a model an illustrious statue of Lysippus whose mouth and chin was rust-eaten or unfinished, would he, unwilling to take the pattern of this part from some other workman, think it better to imitate a disfigured and imperfect face than to give up the model to which he had devoted himself and supply what was lacking from the statue of another workman?

No.—"As we can," the adage runs, "since we may not as we will."

Bu.—That adage would be better quoted by those, Nosoponus, who make good from other writers the deficiencies of Cicero;

[1] Miserable imitator.

for they, though they would prefer to follow him alone either
because it is easier or because no one speaks more happily than
he, borrow from others when necessary. How can we gain-
say the fact that Cicero's works, as we have them, are not only
so mutilated but also so distorted that if he should come to life,
I venture he would not recognize his own writings nor could he
restore those which have been corrupted by the boldness, care-
lessness and ignorance of copyists and pseudo-scholars (mostly
Teutons according to Politian, but while I am unwilling to
defend them, yet at the same time I think just as many blunders
have been made by certain bold Italian sciolists), not to mention
for the moment, the forgeries and works claiming Cicero as
author under false title. Of this class are the four books on
rhetoric dedicated to Herennius, the work of a man by no
means learned and a stammerer in comparison with Cicero. And
there are among Cicero's orations some which do not seem to
have been written by him, but by some scholar for the sake of
practice in oratory. There has been added recently an oration,
Pro M. Valerio, which is actually full of solecisms and utterly
unlike Cicero. Some read the declamation of Porcius Latro
against Catiline as a speech of Cicero's. Then if we with
devoted minds dedicate ourselves to Cicero alone, intending to
express whatever we find without regard to choice, shall we
not find ourselves in the greatest danger, after long and earnest
exertion, of appropriating and imitating only Gothic words and
Teuton solecisms instead of Ciceronian flowerets?

No.—May the Muses avert that ill!

Bu.—I fear that this may happen to us often while the Muses
sleep, Nosoponus. For more than once have we seen this sport.
How often have they · who thought themselves Ciceronians
laughed at a fragment culled from Cicero with the title of some
German added and called it a barbarian's work! Or, when something composed only the day before was brought out with the
name of Cicero attached and pretence made that an original had
been found in a very old library, how they have worshipped!
How they have adored the divine and inimitable phrasing of
Cicero! What about the fact too that scholars admit there are
inexcusable blunders in Cicero's writings, such as have been
made by learned men in all times, when, absorbed in their subject, they remember rather the preceding thought than the words

and thus it happens that the close of the period does not agree with the beginning? As, for example, in *Diutius commorans Athenis, quoniam venti negabant solvendi facultatem, erat animus ad te scribere,* the writer first thought *volebam* or *statueram,* then afterward *in animo erat* was more pleasing; and, though the words made the same sense, yet they fitted poorly with those which preceded. Further, Aulus Gellius cites a passage from the second book of Cicero's *De Gloria,* in which plainly there is a mistake, assigning some verses from Homer's Iliad to Ajax when there they are spoken by Hector. Shall we try to imitate this too? We must if we imitate him in every point. Once more, there is a tradition that Cicero has said some things which scholars have thought ought not to be imitated; for example, *in potestatem esse,* instead of *in potestate esse.* It is of course possible that a slip of the pen or some other mishap in writing made that *tem* for *te* in the original or that the lazy scribe introduced it in the later manuscripts. Again, in the edict of Marc Antony Cicero condemns as a barbarism, unheard of by the Romans, the word [1]*piissimus* from *pius,* though this word is found in the most approved authors. He likewise criticised as a solecism Antony's use of the phrase [2]*facere contumeliam* just as we say *facere injuriam,* although in Terence—the best representative, if I mistake not, of polished Latinity—Thais speaks thus: *Nam si ego digna hac contumelia sim maxime, at tu indignus qui faceres tamen,* where, I think, *contumeliam* is understood to be repeated. Likewise he refrained from using the words [3]*novissime* and *novissimus,* on the ground that they were poor Latin, though Cato and Sallust did not hesitate to employ them. Aulus Gellius bears witness of Cicero's dislike of this word and many others which were often used by good Latin authors both before and after him. And he is said to have written *ss* whenever a long vowel preceded, as in *caussa, visse, remissi* for *causa, vise, remisi.* Shall we then, following Cicero exactly, refrain from those things which pleased scholars but did not please Cicero or follow those which no scholar would imitate or could excuse?

Hyp.—It is, to be sure, a characteristic of lovers to kiss the blemishes of those they love.

[1] Philipp. XIII, c. 19.
[2] Philipp. III, c. 9.
[3] Aulus Gellius X, c. 21.

Bu.—If he is to be copied exactly, shall we write verses after his example, without the aid of Apollo and the Muses?

No.—I make exception of verse.

Bu.—You surely make exception of a good part of his stock when you except verse. What hinders our making use of this exception at least where he is excelled by others, as in this whole field he is inferior to many, not to say all? How many quotations does he use from Homer, Sophocles, Euripides, poorly translated, in iambic verse, contrary to the practice of the Greeks, and with a freedom which Latin writers of comedy have permitted themselves. If you should wish to do something of the same sort would you fear to make a better and more literal translation, lest you be too unlike Cicero? And does he not mar his prose by mingling with it verses of his own translation that fail to harmonize with the rest of the language? Furthermore, since he constantly inserts in his books verses from Ennius, Naevius, Pacuvius, and Lucilius which smack of that uncouth and uncultured antiquity, will it be a point of honor with you to quote like verses, or rather I should say unlike verses, from Vergil, Horace, Ovid, Lucan, or Persius, whose works have as much less crudeness as they have more elegance and erudition? Do you fear in this to seem unlike Cicero?

No.—Of course we shall vary a little from the model we are trying to reproduce.

Bu.—But why is it necessary to imitate exactly and always, when often it is better to rival and sometimes easier to surpass?

No.—I think that even the Muses themselves will never speak better than Cicero.

Hyp.—Perhaps they could if they tried very hard, writing at night, supperless, near a small lamp.

Bu.—Do not get excited, I beg of you, Nosoponus; for I stipulated, once for all, the right to say with impunity what I pleased. When one is as devoted and pledged to Cicero as we are now, is there not danger that one, blind with love, will mistake faults for virtues, or knowingly will portray even his very faults?

No.—'Ηράκλεις!¹ Faults in Cicero!

Bu.—Yes, unless perchance a solecism is a fault in others and not in Cicero; for, as we have said, scholars have pointed out

¹Hercules!

solecisms in his books. Or unless a slip of memory is not a fault, which too has been pointed out by scholars. Or unless it is not a fault to annoy one's client with immoderate mention of one's own praises, which Asconius Pedianus declares was done in *Pro Milone;* and which was almost always a source of annoyance in Cicero because of his desire, as Seneca most aptly says, of [1]*non sine causa, sed sine fine glorians.* And I do not know in which he was the more intemperate—in boasting of himself or in censuring others. With whatever zeal we may defend these characteristics, we shall not be able to deny that at least in this respect a better model can be found.

No.—Let us leave off talking of personal characteristics and revert to the discussion of strength and beauty of speech.

Bu.—I should gladly do so if the rhetoricians did not declare that one cannot be a good orator who is not also a good man. But reverting, does it not seem to you to be faulty composition for a word following another to begin with the same syllables with which the preceding ended, as it were, carrying back a mocking echo; for example, if you should say, *ne mihi dona donata, ne voces referas feras, ne per imperitos scribas scribas Basso?*

No.—I grant that the collocation is foolish and absurd.

Bu.—But such is quoted from our beloved Cicero: [2]*O fortunatam natam me Consule Roman.*

No.—I have already once made exception of his poetry.

Bu.—In my way of thinking, when once you except this you except the whole of Cicero. But you have not yet escaped. Quintilian quotes for you from Cicero's prose as perfect a collocation, *Res mihi invisae visae sunt Brute*—or if you prefer to pronounce after the fashion of Cicero, *invissae sunt*—not to do injustice to the two molossi in the close of the sentence.

No.—That was in a familiar letter.

Bu.—I do not object to it. I only ask if you think it ought to be imitated. Certainly you will acknowledge that some better phrasing could be made.

No.—Perhaps.

Bu.—Do I recall something in this connection about the clashing of vowels which renders speech open and disagreeable? Has

[1] Boasting not without reason but without end. De brevitate vitae, Cap. V.
[2] Quintilian IX, c. 4. Inst. Orator.

not this too been marked by scholars in Cicero? He was indifferent, you say. I do not deny it, but let us acknowledge that there is something in other writers different or better. And let me inquire, what writer have you known so alert and so fortunate that he has never been caught napping at any point?

No.—Why not? They are men.

Bu.—Among men then you number Cicero?

No.—Sometimes.

Bu.—Do you then consider it better to imitate Cicero napping than Sallust or Brutus or Caesar awake?

Hyp.—Who would not prefer to copy one awake?

Bu.—Did not Vergil imitate Homer, though he corrected many of his faults? Did he not imitate Hesiod so that he sometimes excelled him? Did not Horace imitate the Greek lyric poets, culling from each one what was most beautiful and thus surpassing them all? [1]"*Ego*," he says, "*apis Matinae More modoque Grata carpentis thyma per laborem Plurimum, circa nemus, uvidique Tiburis ripas, operosa parvus Carmina fingo.*" And did he not imitate Lucilius, consciously omitting certain things and designedly taking from others what was more worthy of imitation? Need I mention others? Did Cicero himself draw his marvelous fluency from any one model, or rather did he not by sifting equally together Greek and Latin philosophers, historians, rhetoricians, comic, tragic, and lyric poets, weave and finish that divine style of his? If it behooves us to imitate Cicero in every point, why shall we not imitate this example too?

Hyp.—Bulephorus is speaking sense, Nosoponus.

Bu.—What of this? Did not Cicero himself teach that the height of art was to conceal art? [2]"*Friget enim, et fide caret, ac velut insidiosa timetur oratis, quae significationem artis dedit. Quis enim ab eo non metuat, qui fucum et vim parat animis nostris?*" And so if we should want to imitate Cicero successfully, the fact that we are imitating must carefully be hidden. But he who never departs from Cicero's lines, who follows him in words, figures, rhythms, imitating things unworthy of imitation, as the pupils of Plato imitated their teacher by contracting their shoulders, as the disciples of Aristotle copied a sort of stutter-

---

[1] "I", he says, "as a Matine bee culling the liquid from the pleasing thyme wearily mid groves and on the banks of the tawny Tiber, a tiny minstrel, fashion toilsome lays."

[2] For speech is unconvincing and untrustworthy, and shunned as dangerous, which makes a show of art. Who would not shrink from one who tries to deceive?

ing which he is reputed to have had—will he ever, for the very reason that he shows plainly his desire to imitate, have the credit of speaking his mind or gain any reputation? He may be as fortunate as writers of centos who please perhaps for a little while and only the idlers, but who do not teach or move or persuade. This is his highest praise, "He understands Vergil well, he has fashioned a mosaic with such care."

No.—The more manifest the imitation, the more I shall be regarded a Ciceronian. This is my greatest wish.

Bu.—You are right, if we are seeking eloquence for display, not for use. But there is a very great difference between an actor and an orator. The one needs only to please, the other desires also to profit, provided he is a good man; and if he is not good, he cannot claim the name of orator. Already I have shown, I think, that some things in Cicero ought not to be imitated, that some are wanting, and that some are not as good as can be found in more successful authors. But let us grant that there is no kind of embellishment in which he does not either rival or surpass others: to be sure in some authors one beauty, in others another stands out more prominently on account of its rare occurrence, while in Cicero these are lost in the wealth of ornamentation, just as you will find more easily a certain star which you seek, if the stars are far apart than if the whole sky is studded, or as the individual gems on a garment will impress you less, if you see an entire garment covered with gems.

No.—He who absolutely absorbs all of Cicero can give forth nothing but Cicero.

Bu.—We come back to the same point. I will acknowledge him eloquent who copies Cicero successfully; but he must copy him as a whole and his very faults too. I will put up with that suggestion of emptiness, that stroking of the chin with the left hand, the long and thin neck, the continual straining of the voice, the unbecoming and unmanly nervousness as he begins to speak, the excessive number of jokes, and everything else which in Cicero is displeasing to himself or to others, provided only he copy those other traits too by which he concealed these or compensated for them.

No.—I hope that I may attain this before I die.

Bu.—That is just what I am trying to do, Nosoponus. You see how much he covers in how few words who speaks of Cicero in his entirety. But O Muses! how little of Cicero do those apes bring us, who show us only the surface, or rather the veneer of Cicero by a few words, phrases, tropes, and endings of periods, collected here and there. In this way, formerly, certain ones tried to reproduce the Attic style of oratory; but it mattered not that they were dry, jejune, cold, and always, as the saying is, held their hand under their mantles; they could never in any degree attain either the simplicity, the saneness, or the grace of the writers of the Attic school. With perfect justice [1]Quintilian ridicules those who wished to be considered Cicero's own brothers because they ended a period several times with the words, *esse videatur*—a phrase repeatedly used by Cicero whenever the period was rather elaborately developed, especially in the opening sentences of his early works. And a good many now are very proud and count themselves, as they say, second Ciceros, if the first word of the oration is *quamquam* or *etsi* or *animadverti* or *quum* or *si*, because Cicero begins his *De Officiis* with *Quamquam te Marce fili*, and takes full nine lines for the first sentence; his *Pro lege Manilia* with *Quamquam mihi semper;* that much praised speech, *Pro Milone*, with *Et si vereor, judices;* the twelfth Philippic with *Etsi minime decere videtur;* and also the *Pro C. Rabirio* with *Etsi Quirites;* and several letters in the same way. Probably these persons attribute to Cicero the work dedicated to Herennius because the book begins with *Etsi.* The fifth book of *De Finibus* begins *Quum audivissem Antiochum, Brute.* The *Tusculanae Quaestiones* begin *Quum defensionum laboribus;* and the fourth book of the same work, *Quum multis in locis nostrorum hominum ingenia. Pro L. Flacco* begins *Quum in maximis periculis.* Likewise *Pro Domo suo ad Pontifices* begins *Quum multa divinitus.* Again *Pro Plancio, quum propter egregiam.* The first book of *De Natura Deorum, Quum multae res in Philosophia;* and the *Scipionis Somnium, Quum Multae res in Africa. Pro Rabirio, Animadverti, judices.* Again *Ad Brutus de Paradoxis Stoicorum, Animadverti, Brute. Pro L. Cornelio Balbo* begins *Si auctoritas patronorum; Pro Publio Sestio, Si quis antea judices; Pro Caecinna, Si quantum in agro; Pro Archia Poeta, Si quid est in me ingenii; In Vatinium*

[1]Inst. Orator. X, c. 2.

Testem, Si tua tantummodo Vatini; " To the Knights when he
was on the point of going into exile," *Si quando inimicorum;*
" To the Senate, after his return," *Si P. C. vestris; Pro Marco
Caelio, Si quis judices; De Provinciis Consularibus, Si quis
vestrum, P. C.* What could be more ridiculous and more unlike
Cicero than to confine the introduction of a speech to such words.
as these! If any one should ask Cicero why he began with these
words, he would, I think, make the same reply that in the Blessed
Isles Homer made to Lucian's query as to why he began the Iliad
with the word · μῆνιν (for this question had troubled Grammarians for many ages). [1] " Because," said Homer, " that word at
the moment happened to occur to me " Of like effrontery are
those who think themselves ultra Ciceronians because at different
times they prop themselves on these phrases: *etiam atque etiam*
used for *vehementer; majorum in modum* for *valde; indentidem*
for *subinde; quum* and *tum* whenever there are things of un-
equal weight to join, *tum* and *tum* when equal; *tuorum in me
meritorum. Quid quaeris* for *in summa* or *breviter;* and *Non
solum peto, verum etiam oro contendoque.· Ante hac dilexisse
tantum, nunc etiam amare mihi videor. Valetudinem tuam cura,
et me, ut facis, ama. Non ille quidem vir malus, sed parum
diligens,* in which last phrase Cicero seemed so to delight that
you may find it repeatedly on the same page. Likewise when by
the pronoun *illud* he indicates not what precedes but what soon
follows. And if perchance in his letters Cicero has said occas-
ionally, *cogitabam in Tusculanum,* then he considers himself a
Ciceronian who repeatedly says, *Romam cogitabam,* instead of
what he means, *in animo habebam* or *statueram proficisci Romam.*

Cicero does not date his letters by the year, only by the day of
the month. Then a person will not be a Ciceronian, will he, if
he dates the year from the birth of Christ, which is often necessary and always useful? These same persons do not permit one,
as a courtesy, to put the name of the one to whom he writes before his own; for example, *Carolo Caesari Codrus Urceus salu-
tum.* And they consider it as great a fault if one adds to a
proper name any word of dignity or honor, as " Velius greets
Ferdinand the Great, King of Pannonia and Bohemia." They
cannot pardon Pliny the Younger because he uses the word *suum*
in addressing a letter to a friend, simply because no example of

---

[1] Verae Historiae II.

4

this kind is extant in Cicero. They refuse the title to one who
follows the model which some scholars have borrowed from *The
Duties of Princes* and have recently begun to adopt; viz, to place
at the beginning the main point of the letter which they are preparing to answer, because this has never been done by Cicero. I
have known some to be criticised as guilty of a solecism because
instead of S. D. in the salutation they placed S. P. D., that is,
salutem plurimam dicit, which was said not to be in Cicero. And
some think that even this little thing is Ciceronian, to put the salutation on the back of the letter instead of the front because the
carrier is thus told without omitting the courtesy of salutation
which letter he is to deliver to each person. Such a little thing
causes us to lose the palm of glory? Indeed far from a Ciceronian
is he who uses in the salutation this formula, *Hilarius Bertulphus,
Levino Panagatho totius hominis salutem, aut salutem perpetuam;*
and farther the one who begins his letter *Gratia, pax, et miseri-
cordia a Deo Patre, et Domino Jesu Christo* or instead of *cura ut
recte valeas,* closes it with *Sospitet te Dominus Jesus* or *Incolu-
men te servet Dominus totius salutis auctor.* What peals of laughter, what jeers would the Ciceronians raise at this! And what
offence? Are they not Latin words, beautiful, well-sounding,
even splendid? If you should consider the sense, how much
more there is in them than in *Salutem dicit* and *bene vale?* A
master shows this courtesy to a slave, an enemy to an enemy.
But who would regard *dicit illi salutem* and *jubet illum salvere*
as good Latin if it were not Classic usage? This, at the beginning of the letter. Now, at the close, we say *vale* even to
those whom we wish ill. How much more significance in the
phrases used by Christians, provided we are true Christians!
Gratia implies the voluntary giving up of wrongs done; *pax,*
quiet and joy of conscience because God is gracious; *misercordia,*
varying gifts of body and mind with which the kindness of the
mysterious Spirit enriches his own, and when we wish to express
our hope more clearly that these may be lasting we add *A Deo
Patre et Domino nostro Jesu Christo.* When you hear Father
you lay aside servile fear, admitted into the love of the Son;
when you hear Lord, you grow strong against the strength of
Satan. Nor will he desert you, because he has purchased you
so dearly and he alone is more powerful than all the cohorts of
Satan. What sweeter than these words to one who feels that

these blessings are already his! What more useful than this admonition to one who has not yet entered into this love! And so while in choice of words we are not surpassed, but rather surpass; in sense we far excel. There remains to be considered the element of beauty and fitness which is most desirable. And how much more these modern phrases suit the Christian than the *salutem dicit* and *cura ut valeas* of the Romans!

But you say, "Away with these childish imaginations, for Cicero did not use such phrases." What wonder he did not when he did not know them! How many thousands of things there are in our every day conversation of which Cicero did not even dream? But if he were alive he would use the same phrases. Are we not indifferent imitators if we copy Cicero by the observance of such trivial things as rhythms, tropes, phrases, which pleased Cicero or fell frequently from his lips and neglect so many excellent qualities? Perhaps these things do not interest you, Nosoponus, but, inasmuch as we happened to be talking of imitators of Cicero, it did not seem amiss to speak of them. Such people ought to be equally distasteful to us and to Cicero: because we who are trying to be Ciceronians are drawn by them into jest and gossip and are rated by their stupidity; while Cicero, as we have said before, is dishonored by such imitators just as a good teacher is dishonored by bad pupils or a reputable man by unprincipled children or a beautiful woman by a poor artist. Quintilian understood this when he [1] complained that Seneca was being dishonored by the immoderate zeal of those who imitated merely his faults, causing people who had not read Seneca to judge of him by their writings. Just as none boast more of their teachers and ancestors than the poor pupils and wayward sons, grasping at a reputation from any source since they cannot win it through their own good qualities; so none exult more immoderately in the name of Cicero than those who are most unlike him. I have known physicians markedly unskilled in the art they professed, in order to increase their income, to boast that they were pupils of some celebrated doctor whom they had scarcely seen; and, when asked why contrary to medical practice they gave this or that to a patient, would answer roughly, "Are you more learned than so and so? He is my authority." And yet they imitate practically nothing except

[1] Inst. Orator. X, c. 1.

what ought to be avoided; as for instance, too great sternness and peevishness in answering questioners or too much severity in exacting pay. What feelings do you think that illustrious physician would have toward such pupils?

Hyp.—No doubt he would be very bitter, unless he had absolutely no regard for his reputation.

Bu.—What feelings would the real and genuine pupils of the same doctor have?

Hyp.—Just as bitter, because they would suffer the same reputation as this boastful imposter had established. But if you will permit me to interrupt, I will give you an illustration of this.

Bu.—Certainly.

Hyp.—Some one happens to see Erasmus writing with a reed pen to which is fastened a piece of wood; he begins at once to fasten a stick to his pen and thinks he is writing in the style of Erasmus. But go on.

Bu.—What you say is well said and to the point. But I will resume. Do we not hear fathers scolding their ill-mannered sons, "You disgrace me in the eyes of my fellow-citizens; you have dimmed the images of your ancestors; I am ashamed of such children; if you go on I shall disown you?" Do we not in like manner sometimes hear a man, angry at his brother, declaring that his reputation is injured by the brother's wicked ways? Cicero no doubt feels the same toward his ridiculous apes, and so ought we who desire to be considered γνήσια τέκνα.[1]

No.—In a matter so splendid to be even a shadow is worth while.

Bu.—It may be something worth while for those who are satisfied to be called shadows of Cicero, but I have no desire to be called a shadow even of Apollo. I should prefer to be a living Crassus than a shadow of Cicero. But to return, suppose we assume that some one does copy Cicero exactly in words, figures, rhythms (which thing itself I doubt if many can do), how much will he have of Cicero? Suppose he is as good in imitating Cicero as was Zeuxis in portraying the feminine form. Zeuxis reproduced the form, the coloring, the age and—a sign of the highest workmanship—something of the mood; that is, of grief, joy, anger, fear, intentness, sleep. He who has shown these, has he not reached the limit of what art can do? As far

---

[1] His true sons.

as was possible he put a living life into a mute statue. Nothing
more could be asked of a painter. You recognize the form of
the one who has been painted, you see the age and the mood,
perhaps even the condition of health, and besides, as we have
read, the physiognomist recognizes the disposition, the habits,
and the length of life. And yet how far it falls short of a living
being? What can be seen on the surface is represented; but
since a human being consists of soul and body, how little there
is in this of even one half of him and that the worse? Where
is the brain, the flesh, the veins, the muscles and bones, the
intestines, the blood, the breath and the phlegm, life, movement,
sense, voice and speech, and what belong to man peculiarly—
mind, talent, memory, judgment? Just as these, the chief es-
sentials of man, cannot be portrayed by the painter; so we cannot affect the highest virtues of the orator but must get them
from ourselves. Indeed nothing else is required of a painter
except that he portray what his art professes; but of us something quite different is required if we wish fully to represent
Cicero. If our representation is devoid of life, of action, of
mood, of muscles and bones what could be more indifferent?
Still it will be much more ridiculous, if, by great effort we make
the reader recognize that we have read Cicero because of swell-
ings, of warts, of scars, or some deformity of limb in our representation.

Hyp.—A certain painter of this kind was but recently a source
of amusement to us. He had engaged to paint our friend,
Murius, and since he could not paint the true form of the man,
he looked about if he had anything noteworthy on his body or
clothes. He began in the summer and had already for the most
part finished the picture, had painted a ring which he was wear-
ing, a purse and girdle, and had carefully copied the felt cap
on his head. Then he noticed that on the finger of his left
hand there was a scar; this he represented with studied care.
Then on the right wrist he found a large swelling and painted
that. On the left eyebrow he put some hairs in different direc-
tions. On the cheek too he put a scar, the mark of a wound.
Time went on and he had many sittings. If, when he came, he
saw that the beard had been shaved, he painted a new chin;
again if he saw that the beard had grown out he changed the
chin, because that pleased him more. Between times a slight

fever seized Murius which, as is usual, left a sore on his lip; the painter portrayed this. At length winter came, another cap was put on; he changed the picture. Winter clothing of furs was put on, he painted a new dress. Cold changed the complexion and as usual shrunk the skin, he changed the entire skin. A rheum broke out which affected the left eye and made the nose somewhat larger and very much redder, he painted a new eye and a new nose. If ever he saw him uncombed, he ruffled up the hair. If perchance Murius was sleeping while he painted, he represented him sleeping. If he had taken medicine which caused relaxation, he changed the face. If he could have painted the true and native form of the man, he would not have taken refuge in these incidental things. And so if we imitate Cicero in this way, may not Horace deservedly cry out against us:

[1]*O imitatores servum pecus, ut mihi saepe*
Risum, saepe jocum vestri movere tumultus?

But suppose we have represented Cicero as successfully as the consummate painter can represent his model, where is the mind of Cicero, where the originality so abounding and happy, where the power of arrangement, where the thinking out of propositions, where the wisdom in handling arguments, where the power of persuasion, the felicity, the memory so fruitful and ready, the versatility, where in short that soul breathing even now in his writings, that genius, manifesting such peculiar, subtle power? If these are lacking, how indifferent will be our imitation!

No.—You argue cleverly, Bulephorus, but to what end except to keep young men from copying Cicero?

Bu.—Heaven forbid, Nosoponus! My aim is rather this, that, spurning the foolish harangue of certain apes, we may imitate Cicero, as far as may be, both exactly and successfully.

No.—In this certainly we agree.

Bu.—Unless this be done skillfully, we shall strive diligently but not very successfully and shall become most unlike Cicero. For be assured that there is nothing more dangerous than to

---

[1] Hor. Epis. I, 19. 19.   O imitators, servile band, how often have your efforts moved me to laughter and to mirth.

aim at being the image of Cicero. Misfortune came to the giants in their striving to reach the seat of Jove. Destruction came through challenging the Gods. It is a work full of dangerous chance, to reproduce that divine and superhuman tongue. Another Cicero may possibly be born, but none can be made.

No.—What are you driving at?

Bu.—Because while his virtues are the highest, they are yet nearest to vices. | Furthermore imitation must fail which desires to follow only, not to surpass. The more zealously you aim at the reproduction, the nearer you are to this vice.

No.—I do not quite understand what you mean.

Bu.—I will make you understand. Do not the doctors declare that the best health of body is the most dangerous because it is nearest to bad health?

No.—I have heard so. What next?

Bu.—Is not absolute monarchy very near to tyranny?

No.—They say so.

Bu.—And yet/nothing is better than absolute monarchy without tyranny. | Again, is not great generosity a neighbor to prodigality? And does not unusual rigor border on barbarity?

No.—Yes.

Bu.—And wit and humour, do they not approach the neighborhood of coarseness and levity?

No.—Do not mention other instances. Take it for granted I agree to all.

Bu.—First hear this quotation from Horace:

'*Brevis esse labore,*
Obscurus fio; sectantem lenia, nervi,
Deficiunt, animique; professus grandia turget.

Thus those who aim at the Attic style become dry instead of clever and charming; at the Rhodian, diffuse; at the Asiatic, bombastic. Brevity is praised in the work of Sallust. Would there not be danger of becoming unduly concise and abrupt, if one should try to imitate this with painful precision?

No.—Perhaps.

---

[1] Horace Ars Poetica, 25–27
   I prove obscure in trying to be terse;
   Attempts at ease emasculate my verse;
   Who aims at grandeur into bombast falls.—*Conington.*

Bu.—Adequacy and conciseness of language and argument are exemplified in Demosthenes.

No.—According to Quintilian, yes.

Bu.—If any one should set himself anxiously to work to imitate this, to be a Demosthenean, he would be in danger of saying too little. Isocrates is praised for structure and rhythm. He who strives greatly for this may weary his reader by too much precision of periods and may forfeit confidence by the ostentation of his art. Seneca is praised for fluency. The heedless and enthusiastic imitator runs a risk of becoming redundant and extravagant instead of fluent. If you should anxiously imitate the dignity of Brutus you would probably become austere and repellant; if the charm of Sallust, you might become foolish and trivial instead of pleasing. I have known people to prate weak and inane verses when trying to express that wonderful facility of Ovid. But not to weary you with long illustration, I will speak in general. In some a sublety of argument is prominent. One who is strongly attracted to this runs the risk of becoming either cold or obscure. In others we marvel at the happy disregard of art. One who strives to achieve this will probably fall into a common style of speaking, or rather of prating. In another there is prominent the closest observance of rules. He who strives to follow him may fall into a kind of stage style of speaking. Barrenness is nigh to Attic frugality; loquacity to fluency. In swaying the feelings frenzy is close to sublimity just as pomposity follows close to grandeur and recklessness to confident assertion.

No.—I grant all you say.

Bu.—But there are some of these characteristics which are so prominent in authors that they might be considered faults if they were not offset by allied virtues: for example, in Seneca an abruptness and a profusion of aphorisms are offset by the moral purity of his precepts, the splendor of his themes, the charm of his language; in Isocrates the faults of composition are offset by clearness and weight of thought.

No.—All you have said is true, but I do not yet see what you are driving at.

Bu.—At just this. Inasmuch as there are in the single person of Cicero so many of these qualities, an exact and slavish imitation of him seems dangerous to me, for we cannot imitate the virtues which either adorn or conceal them.

No.—What, pray, do you mean by this?

Bu.—His diction is so fluent that he might be criticised at times as loose and free; so exuberant that he could be called redundant; so rhetorical that he seems a declaimer, at the expense of fidelity seeking the glory of the workman, rather than an orator; so free in censure that he could be held malicious; so immoderate in jesting that as consul he seemed ridiculous to Cato; so flattering that he seems humble; so orderly that by rather severe critics he might be called weak and unmanly. And though we acknowledge that in Cicero these are not faults on account of that remarkably happy nature to which everything he does is becoming, that they are even virtues; yet they are found in him in such a form that before a prejudiced judge they would surely be reckoned as faults. Still he balanced every fault by so many excellent virtues that whoever tries to find fault with anything in Cicero's style is by common consent considered a bold slanderer. We do not hope to imitate these virtues; and if we believe Quintilian, they are inimitable and cannot be gained from example or precept but only from native genius. If native genius is lacking, what sort of imitation will there be of those qualities which we have mentioned? Therefore, we conclude that imitation of no one is more dangerous than of Cicero, not only because he is the greatest orator and most talented (for which reason Horace advises against the imitation of Pindar, citing the fate of Icarus), but also because there are many things in him so perfect that they are very nigh to faults. Hence the danger of failure.

No.—But we agreed that the especially splendid qualities were most fit for imitation; for though we fall short somewhat of our ideal, yet we gain the reputation of correct speech.

Bu.—It is one thing to reproduce the same effects, but another thing to give like effects; one thing to have a rule, but another to be a slave to it and follow nothing else. In short, he fails to reproduce his model who does not reproduce also the qualities which bar criticism. And Quintilian points out that these in Cicero are almost inimitable even by those who are fortunate enough to be geniuses.

No.—I do not admit to the contest any except the most extraordinary and divine geniuses. Add unremitting zeal to this
native ability and there will be hope of imitating Cicero successfully.

Bu.—Perhaps, but so few that they are not worth considering.
You know there are some clever people that distinguish between
imitation and emulation. They say that imitation looks toward
likeness, but emulation looks toward superiority. And so if you
put before you Cicero, entire and alone, with the view not only
of copying him but of excelling him, you must not merely over-
take him but you must outstrip him; otherwise if you wish to
add to his fullness of expression, you will become redundant;
if to his freedom you will become pert; if to his jests you will
become scurrilous; if to his style you will become a poet instead
of an orator. Therefore, if you should desire to equal Cicero,
you would run the risk of speaking worse because you cannot
attain, though doubtless you have attained other things, the
divine virtues of this man with which he offsets those things
which are either faults or very nigh to faults; and if you try to
surpass him also, even if you equal him in those things for which
you have native ability, yet whatever you add will be faulty,
since it seems truly to have been declared that nothing can be
added to Cicero's eloquence, as in the case of Demosthenes
nothing can be subtracted. You see, Nosoponus, the risk.

No.—The risk does not at all frighten me provided at last I
may attain the name, Ciceronian.

Bu.—If you scorn all I've said, there is another cause for
anxiety, which disturbs me more, if it will not bore you to listen.

No.—It is your privilege.

Bu.—Do you think the man deserves to be called eloquent
who does not speak appropriately?

No.—Not at all, inasmuch as this is the first requisite of an
orator.

Bu.—Whence is true propriety? Is it not partly from the subject, partly from the character of the speaker and the listener,
partly from place, time, and other circumstances?

No.—Certainly.

Bu.—Furthermore do you not expect a Ciceronian to be an
illustrious orator?

No.—Why not?

Bu.—Then one will not be a Ciceronian if he discourses in the theater on the paradoxes of the Stoics and on the subtilities of Chrysippus; or if he indulges in witticisms in the presence of the Areopagites when a man is on trial for his life; or if he speaks of cooking in words and figures of the tragic poets.

No.—He will be as ridiculous an orator as if in tragic dress he danced in the Atellan farce; or put a yellow robe on a cat, as the saying goes; or purple upon the ape; or adorned Bacchus or Sardanapalus with the skin of a lion and the club of Hercules. For the deed merits no praise, however magnificent in itself, if it is out of place.

Bu.—Exactly so. Therefore, Cicero, who in his own age had no rival, would not have excelled if he had spoken in like fashion in the age of Cato the Censor, of Scipio, or of Ennius.

No.—Ears accustomed to harsher sounds would not have suffered, to be sure, that ornamental and rhythmical kind of diction. For|their speech corresponded to the manners of their times.

Bu.—Then you say that style is the dress of the ideas?

No.—Yes, unless you like better to call it the picture.

Bu.—Well, a dress which is becoming to a boy is not becoming to an old man; one suitable for a woman is not suitable for a man; what is meet for a wedding is not meet for a funeral; nor would fashions of a hundred years ago be approved of today.

No.—No, they would be received with general hissings and laughter. Look at the dress of the court ladies and nobles in pictures painted perhaps sixty years ago. If anyone should appear anywhere in public now in this dress, boys and knaves would throw rotten apples at him.

Bu.—You speak the truth, indeed. For who now would endure respectable women to wear horns, pyramids, very tall cones standing out on their heads, foreheads and temples bald, hair skilfully plucked almost to the middle of the head; and men to wear bulging caps with great tails hanging down, borders of clothing notched, swelling humps on the shoulders, hair shaved the width of two fingers above the ears, garments far too short to extend to the knees scarcely covering the loins, high topped boots with silver chains bound round from knee to heel. Nor at that time would have been less curious the dress which is now considered respectable.

No.—We agree about dress.

Bu.—Will you not grant that Apelles, who was counted the best painter of his age would be said to paint badly, if he should return now and should paint the Germans as he formerly painted the Greeks, and kings as he formerly painted Alexander?

No.—Badly because inappropriately.

Bu.—If one should paint God the Father in such a dress as Apelles painted Jove or Christ as he painted Apollo, would you accept the picture?

No.—Not at all.

Bu.—What if some one should today portray the Virgin Mother as Apelles portrayed Diana, or the Holy Virgin as he painted Venus Anadyomene celebrated in all literature, or Saint Thekla as he painted Lais, would you say that he was like Apelles?

No.—I suppose not.

Bu.—And if anyone should adorn our temples with statues like those with which Lysippus adorned the temples of the Gods, would you say that he was like Lysippus?

No.—I should not.

Bu.—Why not?

No.—Because the statues would not fit the subjects.   I should say the same if any one should paint an ass in the guise of a gazelle or a hawk with the figure of a cuckoo, even if he should expend in other respects the greatest care and skill on the picture.

Hyp.—Nor should I call him a clever painter who would make a deformed man beautiful.

Bu.—What if he should in some other way show great artistic power?

Hyp.—I should not say that the picture was void of art but that it was untrue.   For he could have painted it otherwise if he had wished but he preferred either to flatter his model or to make sport of him.   Come now, do you think him an honest workman?

No.—He certainly has not shown that he is.

Bu.—Then do you think him a good man?

No.—Neither a good workman, nor a good man, since, indeed, it is the height of art to represent things as they are.

Bu.—To do this, there is no especial need of Ciceronian eloquence; for our rhetoricians grant to eloquence the license to lie, to exalt the lowly, to cast down the haughty (which surely is a kind of legerdemain) to steal by strategy into the minds of the listener, and finally by appealing to the emotions—which is a kind of sorcery—to force conviction.

No.—True, when the listener deserves to be deceived.

Bu.—But let us omit these more irrelevant things. It is enough for my purpose that you do not approve of the inappropriate dress, that you condemn the flattering picture.

No.—But what end have these Socratic importations (εἰσαγωγαί) of yours in view?

Bu.—I was plainly coming to this point, namely, that we agree in thinking that Cicero speaks best of all.

No.—We do.

Bu.—And that this most noble name of Ciceronian is not deserved unless one can speak as Cicero does.

No.—Precisely.

Bu.—And that he does not even speak well whose language is inappropriate.

No.—We agree in that too.

Bu.—Further, that we speak fittingly only when our speech is consistent with the persons and conditions of present day life.

No.—Of course.

Bu.—Well then, do the present conditions agree with those of the time when Cicero lived and spoke, considering our absolutely different religion, government, laws, customs, occupations, the very face of the men?

No.—No, not at all.

Bu.—What effrontery then would he have who should insist that we speak, on all occasions, as Cicero did? Let him bring back to us first that Rome which was; let him give us the Senate and the senate house, the Conscript Fathers, the Knights, the people in tribes and centuries; let him give back the college of augurs and soothsayers, the chief priests, the flamens and vestals, the aediles, praetors, tribunes of the people, consuls, dictators, Caesars, the assemblies, laws, decrees of the senate, plebiscites, statues, triumphs, ovations. thanksgivings, shrines, sanctuaries, feasts of the gods, sacred rites, gods and goddesses, the Capitol, and sacred fire; let him give back the provinces, the colonies, the municipal town, and the allies of the city which was mistress of the world. Then, since on every hand the entire

scene of things is changed, who can today speak fittingly unless
he is unlike Cicero? Therefore, it seems to me that our argument brings us to a different conclusion. You say that no one
can speak with propriety unless he copy Cicero; but the fact
itself convinces us that no one can speak well unless he wisely
withdraw from the example of Cicero. Wherever I turn I see
things changed, I stand on another stage, I see another theater,
yes, another world. What shall I do? I, a Christian, must
speak to Christians about the Christian religion. In order that
I may speak fittingly, shall I imagine that I am living in the
age of Cicero and speaking in a crowded senate in the presence
of the senators on the Tarpeian Rock? And shall I borrow
words, figures, rhythms from the orations which Cicero delivered
in the Senate? I must address a promiscuous crowd in which
there are young women, wives, and widows; I must speak of
fasting, of repentance, of the fruits of prayer, the utility of alms,
the sanctity of marriage, the contempt of changing things, the
study of the Divine Word. How will the eloquence of Cicero
help me here to whom the themes as well as the vocabulary
were unknown? Will not an orator be cold who sews, as it
were, patches taken from Cicero upon his garments?

I shall not repeat rumors but what I have heard with my own
ears, seen with my eyes. There flourished when I was in Rome
Petrus Phaedrus, most celebrated in eloquence, and Camillus,
younger but greater in power of expression, save that Phaedrus
had already gained the height of this distinction. But neither
of these, if I am not mistaken, was a Roman by birth. Now an
invitation was extended to any one who would speak of the
death of Christ on the holy day which they call the day of
preparation, in the presence of the Pope. Some days before I
was invited by some learned men to listen to this oration. "Be
sure to be there," they said, "now at last you will hear how
Roman speech sounds on Roman lips." I went eagerly, I stood
next to the platform, not to lose anything. Julius II was present
in person, a thing which very rarely happened, on account, I
think, of his health. A crowded assembly of cardinals and
bishops was there and many scholars who were then living in
Rome, besides the common throng. I shall not mention the
name of the speaker, lest I should seem to cast reflection on a
respectable and learned man. He thought as you do now,

Nosoponus, and was no doubt a candidate for Ciceronianism. The introduction and peroration, longer almost than the real sermon, were occupied in proclaiming the praises of Julius II, whom he called Jupiter Optimus Maximus holding and brandishing in his powerful right hand the three-cleft and fatal thunderbolt and causing by a mere nod whatever he wished. All that had been done in France, Germany, Spain, Portugal, Africa, and Greece, he declared, had been done by the will of Julius alone. So spoke at Rome a Roman in Roman tongue and Roman style. But what had this characterization to do with Julius, the high priest of the Christian religion, vice-gerent of Christ, successor of Peter and Paul? What with cardinals and bishops performing the duties of the other apostles? Could any theme be more sacred, more real, more wonderful, more sublime, better fitted to move the feelings than the one which he had undertaken to present. Could not any man, furnished with any kind of eloquence on this subject, move even men of stone to tears? This was the plan of the discourse:—first to depict the death of Christ as sad, then, with a turn of words, to describe it as glorious and triumphant intending of course to exhibit to us an example of Ciceronian δεινώσεως[1] by which he could sway the minds of the listeners in any way he wished.

Hy.—Well, did he succeed?

Bu.—To be honest, I wanted to laugh when he gave expression to that tragic feeling which rhetoricians call πάθη.[2] I did not see a single man in that whole assembly a whit sadder when he enlarged with all the strength of eloquence upon the undeserved punishments of the innocent Christ. Nor again any one a bit more joyful when he was wholly absorbed in portraying to us that death triumphant, praiseworthy, and glorious. He called to mind the Decii and Quintus Curtius who had sacrificed themselves for the safety of the Republic; Cecrops, Menoetius, Iphigenia, and several others to whom the safety and dignity of their fatherland had been dearer than life itself; he deplored too very dolefully that, while gratitude had been shown by public decrees to brave men who had aided the Republic at their own risk—to some by a golden statue erected in the forum, to others by divine honors decreed—Christ in return for his

---

[1] Effectiveness.
[2] Pathos.

benefactions at the hands of the ungrateful Jews had borne the cross, enduring hardships and the deepest disgrace. And thus he deplored the death of that good and innocent man who merited the best from his race as he would have deplored the death of Socrates or Phocion, who, though they had committed no crime, were compelled through the ingratitude of their fellow-citizens to drink the hemlock; or of Epaminondas who on account of his brilliant campaigns was compelled to plead for his life before his people; or of Scipio who after so many services to the Republic went out to exile; or of Aristides whom the people of Athens ordered to go into exile offended because he was called just on account of his great integrity of character. I ask what could be more unconvincing or more inappropriate than this? And yet in strength he emulated Cicero. But no mention of the secret plan of the omnipotent Father to redeem the human race from the tyrany of the devil by the unparalleled death of his only son nor of the mysteries—what it is to die with Christ, to be buried with him, with him to rise again. The suffering of the innocent Christ was deplored; the ingratitude of the Jews held up to scorn; but no mention of the ill-will and ingratitude of those of us who, though thus redeemed, thus enriched by so many blessings, and called forth to such happiness through unheard of kindness, in return, so far as in us lies, crucify him by returning to the tyranny of Satan, becoming slaves to avarice, luxury, ambition, given more to this world than ever were the heathens, to whom God had not yet opened up this celestial philosophy. When he was struggling to transport us with joy, I wished rather to weep upon hearing the triumphs of Scipio, of Paulus Aemilius, of Caius Caesar and of the deified Emperors compared with the triumph of the cross. If he had wished to glorify Christ, he ought to have emulated the apostle Paul rather than Cicero, who exults, is lifted up with pride, conquers, triumphs, looks from above with disdain upon all things earthly whenever he touches upon the preaching of the Cross. But why make a long story? In so Roman a fashion spoke that Roman that I heard nothing about the death of Christ. And yet, he was a most ambitious candidate for Ciceronian eloquence and seemed to the Ciceronians to have spoken wonderfully, though he said almost nothing on the subject which he seemed

neither to know nor to care for, nothing to the point, and moved
no one's feelings. He merited only this praise that he had
spoken like a Roman and had reproduced something of Cicero.
The speech could have been approved as a specimen of talent
and genius, if it had been delivered by a school boy; but what
good was it for such a day, before such auditors, and on such
a theme, I pray?

No.—You will not tell the name of the speaker?

Bu.—I prefer not, for I have not intended to cast aspersion
upon the name of any but to show an error to be avoided which
deceives not a few today under the shadow of a splendid name.
This mistaken idea is of interest to us, Nosoponus; the name
of the man of whom I have told the story matters not at all.
Moreover, this misapprehension also concerns the glory of
Cicero, whom I see you favor beyond measure, whom all the
learned men of the world justly favor; for these apes not only
exert a harmful influence upon youth but also dishonor Cicero
by the help of whose name they glorify themselves though they
are anything but Ciceronians. Just as men dishonor St. Benedict by boasting themselves Benedictines when in dress, in title,
and in life they approach nearer Sardanapalus than St. Benedict;
and St. Francis—that man incapable of ill-will—when they boast
of his name though they represent in their characters more
nearly the Pharisees; and St. Augustine when they say that
they are Augustinians though they are far removed from the
doctrine as well as the piety of so great a man; and possibly
Christ when they have nothing of him except the title: so men
cast a blot on the fame of Cicero who have nothing on their
tongues except Cicero and Ciceronians, when none are farther
from the eloquence of Cicero than they. Wonderful how they
criticise the crudeness of St. Thomas Aquinas, of Duns Scotus,
of Durandus, and such men! And yet in all fairness these men,
though they boast themselves neither eloquent nor Ciceronians,
are more Ciceronian than those who demand to be considered
not only Ciceronians but even Ciceros.

No.—Strange things you tell.

Bu.—Truth is not strange. Do you not acknowledge that
he who has great versatility is very like Cicero?

No.—Yes.

5

Bu.—┼Two things are conducive to good speaking: that you
know your subject thoroughly, and that the heart and feelings
furnish words.

No.—That indeed Horace and Quintilian teach, and it is very
true regardless of authority; therefore I shall not attempt to
deny it.

Bu.—Whence then will he get the name of Ciceronian who
speaks of things which he neither knows thoroughly nor pursues
heartily and, I might say, which he clearly neglects and hates?

Hyp.—This is indeed a hard question. For how could a
painter, however clever a workmen, paint the figure of a man
whom he had never looked at carefully and perhaps had never
even seen? And too, you can scarcely make workmen of this
class express the thing skillfully, unless they are delighted with
the subject.

Bu.—This then must be the particular care of the Ciceronians
that they know the mysteries of the Christian religion and read
the sacred books with as much zeal as Cicero read those of the
philosophers, poets, augurs, historians, and jurists. It was because of his thorough knowledge of these things that Cicero
was Cicero. If we do not touch the laws, prophets, histories,
commentators of our religion; if we spurn and shrink from them,
how pray shall we be Ciceronians? Another point, you must
speak before Christians on a secular subject—the electing of a
magistrate, marriage, concluding a treaty, or undertaking war.
Of these things shall we Christians speak in the same way as
heathen Cicero spoke to the heathen? Are not all our actions
gauged by the rules of Christ from which if our speech departs
we shall be neither good orators nor good men?

Further, if the Ciceronian utters no word except from his dictionary, what will he do when the changes of time have brought
new words, for he will not find those in the books of Cicero nor in
his own word list? If, whatever is not found in his books is dis-
carded, in spite of the fact that so many of his works have been
lost, see how many words we shall shun as barbarisms which
have been handed down by Cicero, and how many which he would
have used if he had needed to speak on subjects of this kind!
Never in Cicero did we see *Jesus Christ*, the *Word of God*,
*Holy Ghost, Trinity, gospel, evangelist, Moses, prophet, penta-
teuch, psalms, bishop, archbishop, deacon, sub-deacon, acolyte,*

exorcist, church, faith, hope and love, The Trinity, heresy, symbol, the seven sacraments of the church, baptism, baptizer, confirmation, eucharist, extreme unction, repentance, sacramental confession, contrition, absolution, excommunication, church burial, mass, and other innumerable things in which consist the whole life of Christians. These are always coming up. No matter of what one tries to speak, they thrust themselves upon one. What shall we do? Whither shall our painfully precise Ciceronian turn? Shall he use *Jupiter Optimus Maximus* for the *Father of our Lord?* For the *Son,* shall he say *Apollo* or *Aesculapius?* For the *Queen of Virgins,* shall he say *Diana?* For *heathen, public enemy?* For the *church* shall he say *sacred assembly* or the *state* or the *republic?* for *heresy, faction?* for *schism, sedition?* for *Christian faith, Christian persuasion?* for *excommunication, proscription?* for *to excommunicate, to devote to the Furies* or what will be more satisfactory to some *to forbid water and fire?* for *apostles, embassadors* or *couriers?* for the *Roman Pontiff, Flamen of Jove?* for an *assembly of cardinals, conscript fathers,* for a *generous synod,* the *Senate* and *People of the Christian Republic?* for *bishops, defenders of the provinces?* for the *elections of the bishops,* the *comitia?* for the *synod's ordinances,* the *decree of the senate?* for the *Pope,* the *chief prefect of the state?* for *Christ the head of the Church,* the *highest guardian of the Republic?* for the *devil, sychophant?* for *prophet, soothsayer* or *diviner?* for *prophecies, oracles of the gods?* for *baptism, dipping a victim?* for *mass, a sacrifice?* for *consecration of the Lord's body, consecrated bread?* for the *eucharist,* the *sanctifying of bread?* for the *priest, a sacrificing priest* or a *master of the sacrifices?* for a *deacon, a minister* or *priest of the curia?* for the *grace of God, munificence of the Divine Will?* for *absolution, manumission?* You see how few of the innumerable throng of like words I have mentioned. How will the candidate for Ciceronianism act in such a case? Will he keep silent or will he change to words acceptable to Christians?

No.—What else?

Bu.—Let us then imagine an example. This thought, *Jesus Christ, the Word, and Son of the Eternal Father, according to the prophets came into the world and was made man; of his own will he suffered death and redeemed his church; turned the wrath of the offended father from us; reconciled us to Him so that, justified by the grace of faith and freed from tyranny, we are brought into the church and, persevering in the communion of the church, after this life we reach the kingdom of heaven,* a Ciceronian would express thus: *The interpreter and son of most excellent and mighty Jove, preserver and king, in accordance with the response of the soothsayer, flew down from Olympus to earth and, assuming the shape of man, sacrificed himself voluntarily to the shades below for the safety of the Republic and thus freed the state; he extinguished the lightning of most excellent and mighty Jove which flashed about our heads, restored us to his favor so that we, rendered innocent by the wealth of persuasion and freed from the mastery of a deceiver, are admitted into the state; and if we persevere in the fellowship of the Republic we shall gain the highest happiness, when the fates shall have called us from this life, into the society of the Gods.*

No.—You are surely jesting, Bulephorus.

Bu.—I call to witness our beloved Goddess πειθώ[1] that I am treating a serious subject. Suppose occasion arises for a discussion of the most difficult questions in our dogmas, how much of illumination will the discussion have if it proceed by the help of such petty figures? What else but smoke shall I add to the darkness of the subject matter? How often will the reader come to a standstill at difficulties? But suppose up to this point I ape Cicero, what will I do when the theme demands the testimony of the divine scriptures? When something must be cited from the teachings of the decalogue, shall I simply add "Read the law?" When there shall be need to pronounce an ordinance of the synod, shall I add, "Read the decree of the Senate?" When something must be related from the prophets or apostles, will it be enough to say, "Read the testimony?" These are Cicero's regular phrases. And so I shall evade the subjects lest I contaminate Ciceronian diction with words that are not Ciceronian?

No.—How now? Do you advise us to use the phrases of Thomas Aquinas and Duns Scotus?

Bu.—If propriety is an essential, it is better in speaking of sacred things than to copy Cicero. And yet there is a certain happy mean between the Scotists and the extreme Ciceronians.

---

[1] Persuasion.

It does not necessarily follow that all Latin is bad which is not found in Cicero: for, as it has been said often already, his works are not all extant; he did not treat of all subjects of his own time; nor did he know or discuss subjects peculiar to our time. Finally, in propriety and elegance of language Marcus Varro equals Cicero and Caius Caesar surpasses him, for Cicero was not the author and parent of the Roman speech. He was a very great orator and a pleader in civil cases of the first rank, but in some other things he was of the second rank—an indifferent poet, rather a poor translator from the Greek, of uncertain promise in other fields. If I should have to speak of matrimony, a state which is quite different from what it was formerly and a subject upon which Cicero has left us nothing, should I hesitate to choose thoughts and language from Aristotle, Xenophon, Plutarch, the Bible, Tertullian, St. Jerome or St. Augustine for fear of seeming not much of a Ciceronian? And if there is need of teaching on a rural theme, shall I have no right to take what I please from Vergil, Cato, Varro, Columella?

If newly coined words are considered barbarisms, every word was once a barbarism. How many new words will you find in Cicero himself? Especially in those books in which he treats of rhetoric and of philosophy? Who before Cicero heard of *beatitas* or *beatitudo?* What does *finis bonorum* mean to the Latins, though in Cicero it signifies the highest good, or that in which one expresses the highest happiness? How does *visum,* and *visio, species, praepositum,* and *rejectum* sound to us? How would *occupatio, contentio, superlatio, complexio, traductio, frequentatio, licentia, gradatio, status,* and *constitutio, judicatio, continens, firmamentum, demonstrativum genus, inductio, propositum, aggressio, insinuatio, acclamatio* sound to Latin ears? Or innumerable other words, unheard of, before by the Latins, which he either dared to coin or to use in such a new sense that the Roman people did not recognize them? He did not hesitate to do this, in spite of protestation, when he translated the doctrines of Grecian philosophers; he also naturalized in Latin several foreign words in order to explain the content of the rules of the rhetoricians by specific words formed for this special purpose; yet we think it a crime, if in handling new themes we use a few new words? There is no art to which we do not grant the right of using its own vocabulary: the grammarians may say, *supine* and *gerund;* the mathematicians may say *sesquialteral* and *superbipartient;* the farmers and mechanics have vocabularies adapted to their arts. Shall we then confound heaven and earth, if we explain the mysteries of our religion in language peculiar to it? Since the Christian religion first came to us from Palestine, Asia Minor, and Greece, some Hebraic and many Greek words were carried in along with these ideas themselves; for example, *osanna, amen, ecclesia, Apostolus, Episcopus, catholicus, orthodoxus, hereticus, schisma, charisma, dogma, Chrisma, Christus, baptizo, Paracletus, Evangelium, evangelizare, Evangelista, proselitus, catechumenus, Exorcismus, Eucharistia, symbolum, anathema.* The first priests of the Christian religion in order to disseminate their sublime doctrine used ὁμούσιος which we translate *consubstantialis* and *fides, gratia, Mediator,* and others which either were entirely new to the Latins or used in a different sense. Then is being called Ciceronian of so much consequence that we are absolutely silent about things of which we above all others ought to speak? Shall we abstain from words of the Apostles and from those brought into currency by our fathers which are even now in good repute and contrive others in their place? No, indeed. The Greeks introduced *honey, pepper, mustard* into their language, the Romans did the same. Shall we shrink from those words which have come to us along with that divine religion through Christ, the apostles, and the Holy Fathers, and take refuge in Cicero, intending thereafter to borrow words from him, εν τῇ φακῇ μύρον[1] as the Greeks say? If any one should dispute with us seriously, he would very quickly say that the majesty of the Christian religion is marred by the words, figures, and rhythms of Cicero. But I do not agree, for elegance and terseness of speech pleases me always. You may say that he does not speak Ciceronian who, a Christian among Christians, speaks on a Christian theme as Cicero, a heathen among heathens, spoke on a heathen theme; but I say that if Cicero were alive now and endowed with such genius as he was then, with such skill of speaking, with such knowledge of our times as he had of his own, if he were inflamed with such zeal toward the Christian state as he showed for the Roman City and the majesty of the Roman name, he would speak today as a Christian among Chris-

---

[1] Perfume on pulse.

tians. He who can do this may step forth and we shall gladly dub him a Ciceronian if he longs for the name. Cicero, if he were alive today would not consider *God the Father* less elegant than *Jupiter Optimus Maximus,* or *Jesus Christ* less pleasing to the ear than *Romulus* or *Scipio Africanus* or *Quintus Curtius* or *Marcus Decius;* nor less splendid would he think the name of the Catholic Church than that of the Conscript Fathers, the Knights, the Senate of the Roman people. He would say with us *faith in Christ,* he would call those out of Christ *infidels,* he would say *The Holy Comforter, The Holy Trinity.* I offer proofs for my statements. Did the desire of elegance hinder him from using the set phrase rather than rhetorical Latin in the *Philippics* when he was reciting the formula of the senate's decree? Does he not use in *Topics* legal terms very different from the language of the rhetoricans? Would he have spurned words peculiar to our religion?

No.—Your proofs seem convincing.

Bu.—Furthermore, does not the beauty of language in great measure depend upon figures and allusions? Where does Cicero get these? Is it not from Homer, Euripides, Sophocles, Ennius, Lucilius, Accius, Pecuvius, Naevius, from the philosophers and the historians?

No.—I grant that without these ornaments, speech is mean and common. With them it becomes admirable.

Bu.—What if we should borrow as he did from Vergil, Horace, Ovid, Seneca, Lucan, Martial, would we be unlike Cicero to that extent?

No.—That is granted, perhaps reluctantly; for the antiquity of those whose words he quotes has a sort of majesty in Cicero.

Bu.—How comes it then that we think the whole oration defiled if from the most ancient prophets, from Moses, the psalms, the Gospels and apostolic letters we seek the adornments which Cicero sought as a heathen from the heathens? Is it admirable to borrow from Socrates, but blameworthy to borrow from the proverbs of Solomon? Does Solomon compare unfavorably with Socrates in our estimation? Will the oration be made brilliant by a word from Pindar or Horace and defiled by an appropriate one from the sacred psalms? Are weight and dignity added to an oration by introducing a thought from Plato and the charm destroyed by a thought of Christ from the

Gospels? Whence these absurdities? Do we admire the wisdom of Plato more than the wisdom of Christ? Are the books revealed by the Holy Spirit mean in comparison to the writings of Homer, Euripides, or Ennius? But let us make no mention of the Holy Spirit in this connection lest we seem sacrilegious. History, if you take away fidelity deserves not the name of history. Compare, if you will, the story teller, Herodotus, with Moses; compare the story of the creation of the world beginning from Egypt with the stories of Diodorus; compare the books of Judges and Kings with Livy who often contradicts himself, to say nothing of his untrustworthiness; compare Plato with Christ; the εἰρωνείας[1] of Socrates with the divine oracles of Christ; the psalms so spiritual with the eulogies of Pindar; the songs of Solomon with the ditties of Theocritus. Whether you look at the authors or the subjects, there is no resemblance. Divine wisdom has an eloquence of its own and no wonder if somewhat different from that of Demosthenes or Cicero; for one dress becomes the wife of a king, another the mistress of a braggart soldier.

I was going to ask, if any one should begin to compare words, figures, rhythms:—Does *Thessalian vale* sound sweeter to us than *Mount Zion?* Or has *granted by the immortal Gods* more of majesty than *granted by God the Father?* Or is *Socrates, son of Sophroniscus,* more pleasing to our ears than *Lord Jesus, son of God?* Is *Hannibal, the commander of the Carthaginians,* a sweeter sound then *Paul, teacher of the Gentiles?* If you compare the characters; Hannibal strove for the destruction of the Roman people while Paul introduced a religion of salvation. If you compare the words, I ask what is the difference?

Hyp.—If we are willing to acknowledge the truth, there is no difference, save that a deep-rooted fancy has taught us that the words of the one are polished and splendid, of the other ugly and crude.

Bu.—You have hit the nail on the head| But to what is this fancy due?

Hyp.—I do not know.

Bu.—To the facts in the case?

Hyp.—I think not.

Bu.—Do you wish me to speak what is truer than truth?

---

[1] Irony.

Hyp.—You have my permission.

Bu.—I am waiting for our friend's permission here.

No.—Enjoy the right of our bargain.

Bu.—But I fear what I am about to say will not seem very Ciceronian.

No.—That does not matter at all.

Bu.—It is due to paganism, Nosoponus. | It is paganism which influences our ears and minds. We are Christians only in name. The body is baptized in sacred water but the mind is unwashed; the forehead is signed with the cross, the mind curses the cross; we profess Jesus with our mouths, we wear Jupiter Optimus Maximus and Romulus in our hearts. | Otherwise, if we were truly what we are called, what name pray under the sun ought to be more pleasing to our thoughts or our ears than the name of Jesus, through whom we are rescued from so great evil; by whose gracious kindness we are called to such dignity and invited to eternal happiness; at the mention of whose name evil spirits—more than deadly enemies of the human race —tremble and angels bow their heads and knees; whose name is so efficacious that demons flee at the invocation of him, incurable diseases yield and the dead come to life; so kind and friendly that the bitterest calamities are solaced if you sincerely speak the name of Jesus? Are we then persuaded that by this name the luster of oratory is dulled, while Hannibal and Camillus are its true lights? Let us absolutely uproot and cast forth from the mind this paganism. A truly Christian heart let us bring to the reading and we shall see a brilliant star added to our style whenever the name of Jesus Christ is spoken and an exquisite gem when the name of the Virgin Mother, of Peter, or of Paul is used. Added beauty too, we shall see when from the inner sanctuary of the divine writings, from the cruses and ointment boxes of the Holy Ghost, a thought is thrown in appropriately and sincerely; and thus much more dignity will be found in the diction than if there had been added ten thousand phrases from the writings of Ennius and Accius.

Hyp.—Certainly theologians are kept in this way from bringing the charge of heresy.

Bu.—Granted that Cicero's language is full of figures, ours is as full; while in majesty of themes and in trustworthiness we are far superior to him. Only about words does our pagan fancy trick us, does the lukewarm Christian feeling deceive; because those things which are most beautiful by their own nature are distasteful to us; because we do not love—would that we did not hate. For, according to Theocritis, to Love beautiful are even those things which are not beautiful, just as to Hate there is nothing that is not deformed. I come to allusions which if you destroy, you know yourself how you destroy the beauty of speech. Why does one please us very much more, if when pointing out some person in very unsuitable surroundings, he should say "Wild pulse among kitchen vegetables" than if he should say "Saul among the soothsayers" or if, pointing out something said or done at the wrong time, he should say "Perfume on lentils" rather than "A gold ring in a hog's nose," or if, pointing out that not fortune but good conscience is to be trusted, he should say "Hope must be placed in the protection of the sacred anchor" rather than "We must lean upon the solid rock," or if, wishing to act the part of a good man on the stage and to devote himself to the comforts of others rather than to self-aggrandizement, one should say "Nothing is less becoming to a Christian than to play the role of an Aspendian harper" rather than alluding to the word of Paul, "We must look rather to what is lawful than to what is convenient?" If I should try to exhaust such illustrations, it would take a whole volume. I am content to have given a few. How we gape, how we stand stupified if we find an image or even the fragment of an image of the ancient divinities, while we look askance at the images of Christ and the saints! How we marvel at an epigram or epitaph found in some decaying rock or other:— "To the departed spirit of my most beloved wife, Lucia, deprived of life before her time, Marcellus has set up this stone. O unfortunate me! Why do I live!" Notwithstanding we find very often in passages of this kind, not only foolish and pagan sentiments, but also extraordinary solecisms; yet we cherish them, venerating and almost adoring antiquity, while we deride the relics of the apostles. If any one should quote from the Twelve Tables, who would not consider him worthy of the most sacred place? And yet do any of us venerate and cherish the laws inscribed by the finger of God? How we treasure the image of Hercules or Mercury or Fortune or Victory or Alexander the Great or any of the Caesars stamped upon a coin; but smile at them as superstitious who have among their cherished possessions wood of the cross, images of the Trinity and of the Saints!

If ever you have visited the libraries of the Ciceronians at Rome, recall, I pray, whether you saw an image of the crucifix or of the sacred Trinity or of the apostles. You will find them all full of monuments of heathenism. Among the pictures, "Jupiter Slipping into the Lap of Danae through the Impluvium" attracts our attention rather than "Gabriel Announcing the Immaculate Conception to the Holy Virgin;" "Ganymede Stolen by the Eagle" delights us rather than "Christ Ascending into Heaven." Our eyes linger on the portrayal of bacchanalian feasts and festivals of Terminus full of disgrace and obscenity rather than on "The Raising of Lazarus" or "The Baptism of Christ by John." \These are mysteries hidden under, the veil of the Ciceronian name. Under the show of a beautiful name, I assure you, snares are held out to simple minded and credulous youths. We do not dare to profess paganism. We plead as an excuse Ciceronianism. But how much better it would be to be silent!

No.—I was waiting to see how you would advance our cause. But by slipping away into some other channel you have weakened my purpose and frustrated my plans.

Bu.—I said before and I repeat, I am not drawing your mind away from your noble ambitions but I am lifting it to the best. Nor have I mentioned these things because I think that you share my feelings about them, but because I am striving with all my might that we may attain true Ciceronian eloquence; that we may not aim at it diligently with absolutely incorrect ideas and achieve nothing else than that while we desire very much to be considered Ciceronians we become anything but Ciceronians tested by your own premises; viz, that it is a characteristic of Cicero to speak with absolute perfection, that he does not speak even well who speaks inappropriately, and that any diction is cold and dead which does not come from the heart.

No.—How then shall we ever become true Ciceronians? For I shall not be loth to follow your plan if it is better than mine.

Bu.—There is not much else that I could wish for myself or that I could teach you. I can wish for talent and natural ability, I cannot furnish it. | Minds of men have individual bent, \

and this has such power that if they are adapted to one style of speaking by nature they may strive in vain for another.] θεομαχία[1] yields victory to none as the Greeks say.

No.—I know that [2]Quintilian insistently urges the same thing.

Bu.—This then is my first advice, that no one devote himself to copying Cicero whose bent of mind is very unlike Cicero's; for if he does he will come out a monstrosity ·who has lost his own native beauty and has not gained another's. Therefore especial care must be taken to find out the field you are fitted for by nature; and this is desirable also because if there is any faith to be put in Astrology no one can be successful in that with which his horoscope is at variance. One who is destined for letters will never be fortunate in war, and he who is born for war will never succeed in letters. He who is born for wedlock will never be a good monk. He who is naturally˒ a farmer will never have success at court and *vice versa.*

No.—But there is nothing which persistent labor cannot overcome. By human skill we see stone turned into water, lead into silver, brass into gold; through cultivation plants lay aside their wild character. What hinders the genius of man also from being transformed by training and practice?

Bu.—Training improves the pliable nature, wins over the slightly rebellious, and corrects the perverted one; but you will trouble yourself to no purpose, Nosoponus, about a nature antagonistic and set for a different course. ⎸A horse learns to be driven around the race course, he learns˒ a pacing gate; but it would be of no use to lead the oxen to the ring, to call the dog to the plough, or the gazelle to the race-course. Water is perhaps turned into air, air into fire—if fire is ever an elementary substance; but earth is never turned into fire, nor fire into water.

No.—But what hinders us from adapting the language of Cicero to every subject?

Bu.—I acknowledge that there are certain general principles that can be applied to any theme, such as purity, clearness, elegance of expression, order, and such things, but this does not satisfy those apes of Cicero. They demand the absolute reproduction of words—the very thing, which, granting that it could be done somehow or other, in certain allied subjects,

---

[1] A battle with the Gods.
[2] Inst. Orat. X, c. 2.

would be impossible in wholly different subjects. You will acknowledge, I think, that Vergil holds first place among Latin poets just as Cicero among Latin orators.

No.—Yes.

Bu.—Well, if you are preparing to write lyric verse, will you place before you Horace or Vergil?

No.—Horace is the greatest in his class.

Bu.—What if satire?

No.—Horace, with much more reason.

Bu.—What if you are contemplating comedy.

No.—I will go to Terence for a model.

Bu.—To be sure, on account of the great difference of theme.

No.—But the language of Cicero has some peculiar, indefinable adaptability.

Bu.—Exactly the same I could say, "indefinable." Immoderate love for Cicero deceives many, because to adapt the language of Cicero to an entirely different theme is to come out unlike him. But here let me say, it is not necessary to aim at likeness if one may be equal or at least approximate though unlike. What more unlike than the emerald and the gold-bronze! And yet they are equally precious and pleasing. The rose is different from the lily, of different odor; and yet the one equals the other. Have you not often seen two girls of different feature, but both of such beauty that their excellence would make it hard to choose between them? That is not necessarily best which is most like Cicero: for, as I was going to say, no animal in all its members approaches nearer to the figure of man than the ape, and so like is it that if nature had added a voice it could seem a man; again nothing is more unlike man than a peacock or a swan—and yet, I think, you would prefer to be a swan or a peacock rather than an ape.

Hyp.—I should prefer to be a camel or gazelle to being the most beautiful of apes.

Bu.—Tell me, Nosoponus, would you prefer the voice of a nightingale or a cuckoo?

No.—Of a nightingale.

Bu.—And yet the cuckoo approaches nearer to the voice of man. Would you prefer to sing with the larks or to croak with the crows?

No.—To sing with the larks.

Bu.—And yet the voice of the crow is more like that of man. Would you prefer to bray with the asses or to whinny with the horses?

No.—To whinny with the horses, if the fates drove to either.

Bu.—And yet the ass tries, as it were, to speak in human fashion.

No.—But I think that my ability does not differ so much as that from Cicero's. And what is lacking by nature, practice will perfect. But finish your advice to me.

Bu.—You do well to call me back to the path, for my talk was about to slip away in another direction. It is of the greatest importance that we really accomplish our desire of expressing Cicero completely, though he is complete neither in words nor in phrases nor in rhythms; nor indeed are hardly half his works extant as has been explained sufficiently before.

No.—Where then is he complete?

Bu.—Nowhere except in himself. But if you wish to express Cicero exactly, you cannot express yourself. If you do not express yourself, your speech will be a false mirror and will be as absurd as if, by smearing your face with colors, you pretend to be Petronius instead of Nosoponus.

No.—You speak in riddles.

Bu.—I will use more homely phrase. They play the fool who distort themselves to copy Cicero exactly; for it would not be possible, if it were desirable; and it would not be desirable, if it were possible. But he can be expressed exactly in this way: if we strive in our imitation to express not his exact virtues, but as great ones, or it may be greater. Thus it can happen that|he is most a Ciceronian who is most unlike Cicero, that is, who speaks best and most pointedly, though in a different way; and this is not surprising for the environment is now entirely different.| To illustrate—if one should wish to paint an old man whom Apelles had painted in youth he would be different from Apelles in this very thing, if he should paint him in the same way, though the model were now quite changed.

Hyp.—A riddle worthy of the Sphinx, that someone is unlike in that very thing in which he is like.

Bu.—Would not this happen if any one should sing at a funeral as Hermogenes sang at a marriage, or should plead a

case before the Areopagites with such gestures as Roscius made
while dancing in the theatre? But we may be like Cicero.

No.—How?

Bu.—Did he devote himself to the imitation of one person?
No, he strove to copy what was especially appropriate in every
one. Demosthenes was his first but not his only model; nor
did he take him as model in order to copy him exactly, but to
cull the suitable; not to be content to follow, but to choose
and wisely shun some traits and improve upon others and to
imitate those which he approved of in such a way as to surpass
if possible. Besides, the sanctuary of his heart he filled to over-
flowing with the authors of all the branches of knowledge old
and new. He learned by heart the families of the state, the
rites, customs, laws, edicts, plebiscites. Not only he busied himself industriously at the shrines of the philosophers, but also
betook himself frequently into the retreats of the Muses, learning pronunciation from one, gesture from another. He who
does exactly these things will come out very different from
Cicero; he who does like or equal things will earn the name,
Ciceronian.

No.—Speak somewhat more clearly.

Bu.—He who busies himself with the same zeal in the field
of the Christian religion as Cicero did in that of secular things;
who drinks in the psalms and prophets with that feeling which
Cicero drank in the books of the poets; who desires to find out
the decrees of the apostles, the rites of the church, the rise,
progress, and decline of the Christian Republic with such vigi-
lance as Cicero labored to learn thoroughly the rights and laws
of the provinces, towns, and allies of the Roman City; and who
adapts what has been compiled from all these studies to present
themes,—that one can claim with some right the name, Ciceronian.

No.—I do not see the point of all your talk unless it is that
we speak in Christian style, not Ciceronian.

Bu.—What! He is not a Ciceronian to you who speaks
inaptly and is ignorant of the subject about which he is talking!

No.—By no means.

Bu.—But this is the tendency of those who now desire to be
called Ciceronians. We are inquiring into this so that we may

not fall into the same error. There is no reason why one should not speak in a style at once Christian and Ciceronian, provided you acknowledge him a Ciceronian who speaks clearly, fluently, forcibly, and appropriately, in harmony with the nature of the theme, the condition of the times, and the characters. Now some have thought the faculty of speaking well was not due to training but to judgment, and Cicero himself in his *Partitiones* nicely defines eloquence as "wisdom speaking fluently." There can be no doubt that he sought this kind of eloquence. Ye Gods! how far away from this ideal are those who wish to speak, in Ciceronian style, on widely varying themes which they neither know nor care for. That everything which is not in harmony with Cicero seems sordid and faulty is a dangerous and deceitful dream of our minds, to be relegated far from us, if we wish to enjoy that distinction among Christians which Cicero enjoyed among his contemporaries. [1]*Scribendi recte sapere est et principium et fons,* says that most clever of critics. What pray is the fount then of Ciceronian eloquence?—A mind richly instructed in general knowledge with especial care on those subjects about which you have determined to write, a mind prepared by the rules of rhetoric, by much practice in speaking and writing and by daily meditation, and what is the essential point of the whole matter, a heart loving those things for which it pleads, hating those things which it condemns. Joined to all this must be a natural insight, discrimination, and wisdom which cannot be embodied in precepts. How, pray tell me, do these things come to those who read nothing by day or night but Cicero?

No.—But it has been said, and not without shrewdness, that they who work long in the sun take color, and those who sit long in a perfumed dwelling carry the odor of the place with them when they leave.

Bu.—This comparison pleases me very much indeed. They take with them only the coloring of the skin and a whiff quickly vanishing. Those who are content with such glory may sit as much as they please amid the ointment boxes and the rose gardens of Cicero, may bask in his sunshine. I should prefer, to put the good spices into my stomach, to inject them into my

---

[1] Wisdom is the font and source of good writing. Horace, Ars Poet. 309.

veins so that not only I might sprinkle my neighbors with the delicate perfume, but that I myself might feel the glow and might become so animated that upon occasion a word might come forth which would seem the issue of a sane and well-fed mind. For out of the inmost veins, not out of the skin, is born the style which holds the listener, moves him, and carries him where you will. I do not say these things because I think that out of the books of Cicero is gathered a common and pitiable store, but because Cicero alone is not enough to furnish richness of speech on every theme.

What conclusion then, except that we may learn from Cicero himself how to imitate Cicero? Let us imitate him as he imitated others. If he settled down to the reading of one author, if he devoted himself to the copying of one, if he cared more for words than for ideas, if he did not write except in bed at night, if he worried himself a whole month over one letter, if he thought something eloquent which was irrelevant, let us do the same thing that we may be Ciceronians. But if Cicero did not do these things, which we must grant, let us, after his example, fill our hearts with a store of general knowledge; let us care first for thoughts, then for words; let us adapt the words to the sub- jects, not subjects to words; and while speaking let us never move our eyes from that which is seemly. Thus, in short, will the oration be alive only when it is born in the heart and does not float on the lips. The precepts of art let us not ignore, for they contribute most to the invention, disposition, and handling of arguments; and let us avoid those things which either are superfluous or hinder the case; but, when a serious case is to be handled let wisdom hold first place. And in fictitious cases which are handled for the sake of practice, it is best for the arguments to seem as true as possible. Cicero has written that the soul of Laelius breathed forth in his writings; but it is stupid for you to try to write with the taste of another and to take pains that the soul of Cicero may breathe forth from your writ- ings. That must be digested which you devour in your varied daily reading, must be made your own by meditation rather than memorized or put into a book, so that your mind crammed with every kind of food may give birth to a style which smells not of any flower, shrub, or grass but of your own native talent and feeling; so that he who reads may not recognize fragments culled

6

from Cicero but the reflection of a well-stored mind. Cicero had read all his predecessors and weighed carefully what was worthy of sanction or censure in each; yet you would not recognize any one of them in particular in Cicero but the force of a mind animated by the thoughts of them all.

If Cicero's method is not convincing, let us consider an example from nature. Do bees gather the material for their honeycomb from one shrub? Do they not rather fly about all kinds of flowers, shrubs, bushes, with wonderful zeal, frequently seeking from afar what they may store in their hive? Nor is what they bring straightway honey. They fashion a liquid with their organs, and after it is made their own, they give that forth in which you do not recognize the taste or the odor of flower or shrub but a product mingled in due proportion from them all. Nor do the she-goats feed upon one kind of foliage that they may give milk like only to these; but they feed on every kind of leaf and give forth not the juice of herbs but milk transformed from them.

No.—Yet it makes a difference where the bee gathers the liquid, or upon what leaf the she-goat feeds. If, indeed, yew-tree honey is made from the yew-tree, will not likewise the taste of the milk from the she-goat savor of oak leaves and willows?

Bu.—Well, take artists. Do those who seek fame in plastic or graphic art devote themselves to the imitation of only one master or do they take what they please from each for the perfection of art, so imitating that they may possibly surpass? What about the architect? Does he, when preparing to build some great house, take all the details from a single building? Not at all, he selects from many what he finds to his taste, else no great praise would he gain when the spectator recognizes this or that building reproduced. And yet to be a slave to the copy in art is more tolerable than in oratory. What is the reason then that we have devoted ourselves so religiously to Cicero alone? They sin twice who not only set themselves to just one copy but also, being ignorant of rhetorical rules, read no one except Cicero and nothing outside to teach them how to appreciate him. For what profits it to have your eyes fixed on Cicero if you have not skillful eyes? What would it profit me who am ignorant of the art of drawing, if I should look whole days at the pictures of Apelles and Zeuxis? But when you have learned the rules of rhetoric and when some skilled artist has pointed out to you in several of those orations in which Cicero has reached the height of his art the essential elements of his style:—propositions happily devised—their order, division, treatment, enrichment, perfecting seeds of the entire oration in the introduction; the conjunction of the individual parts; his wisdom and judgment which can be appreciated but not learned by rule; when likewise you have seen clearly the discrimination of the orator—what he has included and where, what he has omitted and why, what he has deferred and to what point of the speech; furthermore, in what way he handles the emotions; and lastly, the splendor, range, and ornamentation of his discourse,—then at length you will see wonderful things in Cicero which your busy imitator never sees. For he does not imitate art who does not understand it and no one understands save the artist. A skillfully wrought piece of work fills with some satisfaction even those who are ignorant of art but how little there is which your imitator sees!

No.—From whom do you seek art more properly than from Cicero?

Bu.—I acknowledge it. No one has bequeathed it to us more happily, no one had practiced it more perfectly; and yet Quintilian has taught it with greater care and also in greater detail, because he not only gives rules but also illustrates first principles, development, method, execution, preparation, adding many things which Cicero either has omitted or has but incidentally touched, such as, the way of exciting the feelings, the kinds and use of aphorisms, the methods of amplifying, the formulation of propositions, their division and arrangement, the transposition and uniting of the essential points, the proper way of reading, imitating, writing. But while we ought not to be ignorant of rules, yet we ought not to be pedantic about them, or to be slaves to them, for the anxious observation of rules causes us to speak worse, whereas the business of art is to make us speak better. That skilled teacher has contributed much more than rules. Not only some of the Greeks, but also some of the Romans have tried the same but have not succeeded so well. We must be careful then, Nosoponus, not to think, as some of your friends do, that we may become Ciceronians with no knowledge of rhetoric, simply by constantly reading Cicero. For if they get anything of Cicero, they get only a kind of outer skin, shadow, and breath.

No.—I do not deny, Bulephorus, that there are many such, and their method has never pleased me.

Bu.—There is no personal reference to you. It applies to Hypologus and myself. With this understanding, let us consider, my dear friend, whether, in the first place, it would be proper for us; in the second, whether it would be worth the while to buy with such vigils the honor of the name, Ciceronian?

No.—There is nothing more honorable; and what is honorable cannot be improper.

Bu.—To discuss the propriety: You will acknowledge I think, that Cicero's language would not have pleased the age of Cato, the Censor; certainly it was more ornate and more luxuriant than was agreeable to that age, frugal in life and in speech. Aye, even when Cicero lived, there were men who breathed forth that early severity—Cato of Utica, for example, and Brutus, and Asinius Pollio—who vainly sought in Cicero's eloquence something more severe, less theatrical, more masculine, in spite of the fact that at that time eloquence flourished so mightily in the popular assembly, in the senate, in the courts, that the judges both expected and demanded an ornate and attractive style from the lawyers. If Cicero's style was lacking in manly vigor, do you think it appropriate for Christians, whose every plan looks rather to living virtuously than to speaking ornately and elegantly, from whose lives all paint and theatrical effects ought to be far removed?

But suppose that it is appropriate, what reward for all your toil? The aim of all this work is to persuade. But how much more powerful in persuasion was Phocion than Demosthenes, Aristides than Themistocles, how much more effective Cato than Cicero, who sometimes injured the prisoner by his defence, or aided him by his accusation? I will not linger here over those very magnificently delivered speeches. It is more beautiful to be a Phidias than a keeper of the chest or a cook, though their work is more useful to the Republic than the statues of Phidias. The skill of painters and sculptors is found in delighting the eye; when this is fulfilled their task is done. Eloquence which does nothing but delight is not really eloquence, for it was intended to gain a different end; and if it does not succeed, it ill

becomes a good man. Even granting that the eloquence of
Cicero was useful once, what is its use today? In the courts,
you say? There the case is presented in legal provisions and
formulas by attorneys and lawyers who are anything but Ciceronians before judges in whose eyes Cicero would be a barbarian. Nor is there much more use for him in councils
where individual men state their views to a small group in French
or German. And business of especial importance is done today
in a secret committee composed of scarcely three men and these
almost illiterate whom the rest may consult. Furthermore, even
if today the cases were tried in Latin, who would endure such
a peroration as Cicero made in the cases against Verres, Cata-
line, Clodius, and the testimony of Vatinius? What senate so
amply supplied with time and patience that it would abide the
orations he delivered against Antony, though in these the eloquence is that of an older·man, is less redundant and less
boastful?

Therefore for what useful end, pray, are we securing this
laboriously won eloquence of Cicero? For popular assemblies?
The common people do not understand the language of Cicero;
and in popular assembly no state business is transacted. In
church councils certainly this style of oratory does not belong
at all. What use then is it, unless perchance in embassies, which
at Rome especially are carried on in Latin by force of tradition
rather than from choice and for the sake of display rather than
utility; for in them practically no serious business is transacted,
all speech being spent in words of praise of him to whom you
are sent, in testimony of the goodwill of him by whom you are
sent, and in set common-places. In a word, all this is of such
a nature that you have accomplished a great thing if you have
avoided the appearance of adulation, even though perhaps you
have been really guilty. The response is customarily rather
dull, distressingly prolix, embarrassing to him who is praised
immoderately, mortifying to the speaker and also risky, for he
sweats while reciting what he has learned, is perplexed and sometimes does not know how to proceed either because of forgetful-
ness or confusion. What admiration, moreover, could such
speeches elicit, when they have been learned from some rhetorician so that no reputation comes to our orator except the cour-
age of recitation? Thus at Rome nothing is done except the

exchange of courteous greetings. The serious business is transacted privately by letter and by conferences at which French is
spoken. Then what theater of action will our Ciceronian seek?
He will write Ciceronian epistles? To whom? To the learned;
but they are very few and care nothing about the language's
being Ciceronian provided it is sane, prudent, elegant, and
learned. To whom then? To the four 'Italians who recently
have begun to boast themselves Ciceronians, though, as it has
been shown, there is nothing more unlike Cicero than they, who
have scarcely the faintest trace of him. [1]

Perhaps nothing ought to be despised, however trivial, if it
comes without effort, if it hinders not greater and more important things. But ask yourself whether this reputation ought to
be bought at the expense of sleep, of great toil, perhaps of
health itself, in order to be taken into the list of Ciceronians
by four silly Italian youths.

No.—You do not approve of the study of eloquence then?

Bu.—Cicero does not require eloquence from a philosopher.
Do you think any one among the heathen philosophers weightier
than any Christian?

Hyp.—No, indeed. All the philosophy of the Greeks compared to the philosophy of Christ is a dream and bauble.

Bu.—Then how brazen are we to exact of a Christian Ciceronian eloquence, which is both inimitable and even in a Pagan's
opinion ill becoming a serious man? And it does not follow
that a style is bad because it differs from Cicero's. Nor can it
be too oft repeated that fitness is absolutely essential to good
style. Add to this that any armor which is only for show and
not at hand when the occasion demands is useless. Business
sometimes urges us to write twenty letters in one day. What
will my Ciceronian do in such a case? And again how few
there are now who care for Ciceronian style? What about the
fact too that Cicero has many styles? He has one when, in
relaxed and quiet conversation, he teaches philosophy; another
in the pleading of cases; another in letters where the language
is not studied but even almost careless,—very appropriate for a
letter which follows the turn of familiar conversation. Would
it not be absurd for one to write a letter on a matter of business
as carefully as Cicero wrote the oration *Pro Milone?* And shall

[1] Aonio Palerio, Jacob Sadolet, Peter Bembo, etc.

we put a month's work on a brief note about matters of little importance? Not even Cicero would have bought that eloquence which he displays in court if it had cost him as many vigils as a letter costs us; though in his day the exercise of eloquence in the Republic was great, its study both in private and official life flourishing, and that facility was far 'more easily gained. Rightly was the man ridiculed who tormented himself for days and still was not able to compose the exordium of his oration because he was striving to speak better than he could. There is in Cicero a certain happy, natural ease, and a native clearness. If nature has denied us this, why do we vainly torture ourselves? Why do others, madder far than we, torment themselves in these times, when all the conditions are changed and when there is hardly any practice of Ciceronian speech, with this one desire of being Ciceronians and nothing but Ciceronians?

No.—Your rhetoric is beautiful, but I cannot rid myself of this longing, it has taken such hold of me.

Bu.—From a moderate desire of imitation I do not call you, but imitate only his best; emulate rather than follow; desire more truly to rival than to be exactly alike; work along the line of your natural ability; do not endeavor to make your speech harmonize so with Cicero's that it does not fit your subject. Above all, show no anxiety; for anxiety is always unfortunate and never anywhere more than in speaking. Finally, do not take the matter so seriously that, if you do not succeed, you will count life bitter and not worth living, although you know that many thousands of learned men without this title have attained great reputations in life, and immortality after death.

No.—That is indeed the way I feel now.

Bu.—I too felt that way once but I have recovered from the disease.

No.—How pray?

Bu.—I called a doctor.

No.—Whom, pray?

Bu.—An eloquent, an efficacious one.

No.—Whom, I say?

Bu.—In comparison to whom Aesculapius and Hippocrates are as nothing.

No.—You are playing with me.

Bu.—Than whom no one is more ready, more friendly, more faithful; than whom no one cures more perfectly; he heals one all over.

No.—If you will not give his name, at least give his remedy.

Bu.—Both his name and his remedy you shall know   ὁ λόγος Τῷ λόγῳ has cured me.

Hyp.—You speak most truly.   ψυχῆς νοσούσης ἐστὶν ἰατρὸς λόγος[1]

Bu.—So I have recovered from that disease, Nosoponus. And now, if you wish to take my character for a time, I will play the physician.

No.—I'll play the part.

Bu.—When the paroxysm of the disease was upon me, the doctor spoke to me just as I am now speaking to you. "A false shame," he said, "is overwhelming you" because you cannot endure a taunt common to so many thousands of men.

No.—What taunt?

Bu.—Because you are denied the title of Ciceronian.

No.—This hurts me, I acknowledge.

Bu.—But answer me in the name of the Muses, what Ciceronians can you mention to me, save only Cicero himself? Let us begin with the ancients. In the very long list of orators which Cicero has compiled in the *Brutus* there are scarcely two whom he deems worthy of the title of orator at all, to say nothing of being Ciceronians. Caius Caesar cannot be called a Ciceronian, in the first place because he was contemporary, and in the second place because he aimed at a very different style of oratory, content to speak gracefully and in his own distinctive way. How little there is of Cicero in this! For it is not so commendable for an orator to speak elegant Latin, as it is disgraceful for him to be ignorant of elegant Latin. Then too, Caesar's works are not extant except some letters and the *Commentaries* about the authorship of which there is much dispute among scholars. There is certainly no oration extant, while in this Cicero especially excelled. I may say the same of Marcus Caelius, Plancus, and Decius Brutus, whose letters we have in abundance, thanks to the zeal of Tiro. I may say the same also of Cneius Pompeius, L. Cornelius Balbus, Lentulus, Cassius, Dolabella, Trebonius, Publius Vatinius, Servius Sulpicius, Aulus

---

[1]Reason with reason.
[2]Reason is the physician of a diseased mind.

Caecina, Bithynius, Marcus Brutus, Asinius Pollio, Caius Caesar, and others, fewer of whose letters we have but who were contemporaries of Cicero, so that it is not more fitting for Marcus Caelius to be called a Ciceronian than for Cicero to be called a Caelian. Nor is there any resemblance to Cicero's letters except the clear and natural elegance of the Roman language. You object on the ground that in his letters you have not that complete Cicero whom you set before yourself as model! At this point I would say something of Crispus Sallust, a contemporary of Cicero, but very unlike him in style.

No.—Do not mention those rough, uncombed ancients in whose time eloquence as well as manners had not yet become polished, nor the contemporaries of Cicero, but those who lived after him.

Bu.—Well, does Seneca seem to you a Ciceronian?

No.—By no means, particularly in prose. And the *Tragoediae*, which are esteemed by scholars, could hardly have been written by Seneca.

Bu.—Valerius Maximus?

No.—He is as much like Cicero as a mule is like a man. So different indeed is he that you would scarcely believe he was an Italian or that he lived in that age which he describes. So different is his whole style that you might say he was an African. Never was poetry more labored.

Bu.—What about Seutonius?

No.—Just as different from Cicero as Seneca was, reproducing him neither in words, nor structure, nor clearness, nor ornamentation, nor elegance.

Bu.—Do you consider Livy worthy the honor?

No.—In the first place he is a historian, in the second place he is careless in style, and has been criticised for his Patavinity.

Bu.—I do not dare now to suggest Cornelius Tacitus.

No.—It isn't worth while.

Bu.—Perhaps you will allow Quintilian in your list.

No.—He really strove to be unlike Cicero; but I wish his *Declamationes* were extant, for the writings which we possess have the faintest suggestion of Cicero.

Bu.—But I have one you would not scorn, Quintus Curtius.

No.—He is a historian.

Bu.—Yes, but in his histories there are some orations.

No.—He is a more promising candidate than the others, but nothing, they say, to the swine of Parmeno. He has many tricks of style different from Cicero.

Bu.—If you reject him, you will not accept, I presume, Aelius Spartianus, Julius Capitolinus, Aelius Lampridius, Vulcacius Gallicanus, Trebellius Pollio, Flavius Vopiscus, or Aurelius Victor.

No.—In these there is scarcely anything which you would commend, except historical fidelity. They are so far from deserving the name of Ciceronians that they ill preserve the purity of the Latin tongue.

Bu.— Well, here is 'Probus Aemelius!

No.—He praises fair-mindedly all whose biographies he writes so that you might call him eulogist more fittingly than historian.

Bu.—Perhaps you will accept Ammianus Marcellinus?

No.—Slow of speech, but with style approaching the poetic, when he urges us to give up our captives. I should accept more quickly Velleius Paterculus, and yet I do not deem even him worthy this honor.

Bu.—You will not grant the honor, I suppose, to the compilers of epitomes,—Florus, Eutropius, and Solinus?

No.—I will if any scholar recognizes them as such, but on this ground, because they reflect what they imitate.

Bu.—But I must go back. We have omitted the two Scipios. I know you will not allow the elder to be mentioned here. Perhaps you will the younger?

No.—No, indeed, the censors of this case especially forbid his letters to be read by youths, lest they become Plinians, instead of Ciceronians.

Bu.—But he wrote a pretty clever speech in praise of Trajan.

No.—Very clever, but not Ciceronian.

Bu.—I purposely omit the poets, easily divining your answer, if I should bring forward the most illustrious and charming of all,—Vergil, Horace, Ovid, Lucan, and Martial.

No.—In Horace there is not a trace of Cicero; in Vergil some, though faint. Ovid might be the Cicero of the poets. Lucan is more orator than poet though very different from Cicero. Martial comes very close to the charm of Ovid and something of Ciceronian praise he could have won, if he had not prefaced sev-

¹Cornelius Nepos.

eral of his books with letters—Goodness knows how different from Cicero's!

Bu.—What if I should suggest Lucretius?

No.—At the same time bring forth Ennius and Lucilius.

Bu.—Scholars admire the fair phrases of Aulus Gellius.

No.—Neither his themes nor his language pleases. His speech is affected and verbose, his range of subjects is meagre.

Bu.—Consider Macrobius.

No.—He's exactly the poor little crow of Aesop. From the patches of others he has woven his patchwork, so his own tongue does not speak; and if ever it should, you would think a Greekling were stammering Latin. An example of this you will find in the *Second Commentary on the Dream of Scipio*. All his wisdom is borrowed and as old as Homer.

Bu.—Well, some admire Symmachus who is clever in his letters.

No.—Let them admire him who prefer a labored style.

Bu.—But hold, we have passed Apuleius by!

No.—I shall compare him with Cicero when I may compare a jackdaw with a nightingale.

Bu.—That may be true in reference to his *Golden Ass* and *Florida,* but he approaches Cicero at least in his *Apology.*

No.—Yes, he approaches but still is far behind. But you have forgotten Martianus Capella also, if you care to include such as he.

Bu.—Suppose we take up those who are half Christians. What do you think of Boethius?

No.—A worthy philosopher, not a mean poet, but far removed from Ciceronian.

Bu.—What about Ausonius?

No.—I grant him talent and training, but his style smacks of the pleasure and licentiousness of the court just as does his life: instead of being a Ciceronian, he seems to have designedly spoken in different fashion. If one, therefore, should call him a Ciceronian one would disgrace instead of honor him, just as you would if you should call him a German who wished to be counted a Frenchman even if he were a German.

Bu.—To make a long journey short, let us come, if you please, to the Christians and see if we may find perchance some one who deserves to be called a Ciceronian. I suppose you will approve of Lactantius who is reputed to send forth a *lactean* stream of Ciceronian eloquence.

No.—Reputed yes, but by one who was not a Ciceronian.

Bu.—But this you cannot deny that Lactantius strove for the eloquence of Cicero. The preface of the third book of the *Institutiones* declares this, where intent upon the truth of the Christian philosophy he longs for eloquence, if not Ciceronian, at least approximately Ciceronian.

No.—And certainly he did not try without some success, though he did not attain his desire.

Bu.—How so?

No.—For he said in the very first of the preface of that work: *¹Alioqui nihil inter Deum hominemque distaret, si consilia et dispositiones illius majestatis aeternae cogitatio assequeretur humana.* When did Cicero ever use *dispositiones* for *decreta?*

Bu.—By no means has he become unlike Cicero in his desire to be a Ciceronian. For it is a characteristic of Cicero to emphasize a thing by two words meaning the same, or almost the same. This is the reason for the words, *consilia et dispositiones.* Who knows but that he seized upon the hiatus in *consilia atque* and again in *cogitatio assequeretur* in order to be Ciceronian? Perhaps he had in mind the rhythm too, finishing the clause with the close of a scazon, as in *balneatore* and *archipirata.* Endings of this kind he frequently uses in the same preface, as in the very first sentence, *inhaerere,* and again *instruere possimus,* and soon *apud Graecos, luce orationis ornata,* and *honesta suscepta,* and immediately after *honorasti,* then soon after *nominis tradas,* and *ut sequerentur hortarer,* likewise a little after, *reliquerunt.* That certainly is Ciceronian which frequently ends in a double trochee, as *contulerunt, convocamus, sopiamus, inchoamus;* and once in the close of a period he puts *quaesisse videatur.* This shows that he tried very hard to imitate Cicero. But, with some justice you refuse Luctantius the title of Ciceronian on the ground that he did not bring to the defense of the Christian philosophy the erudition, vigor, and feeling that Cicero brought to the pleading of civil cases.

Bu.—In what order shall I present the rest? Shall Cyprian be first?

---

¹"Otherwise there would be no difference between God and man, if human thought could attain to the plans and disposition of that divine power."

No.—He wrote as a Christian rather than as a Ciceronian.

Bu.—Hilary?

No.—Soho! Nothing like. He is tedious and obscure and raises himself on his Gallic buskin, as they say, dragging with him many words that are not of Ciceronian purity.

Bu.—Sulpicius, I presume, will seem worthy of this honor?

No.—He is indeed more delicate, more pleasing, clearer, and more spontaneous than Hilary, but his language declares him to be a Frenchman. Piety is not lacking but force and dignity are. He has a florid rather than a vigorous style.

Bu.—You will admit Tertullian?

No.—You are jesting. He purposely and consciously hid good thoughts under mean words and was even more rugged than Apuleius himself.

Bu.—Certainly you will not reject that most eloquent and learned St. Jerome?

No.—I recognize in him a man distinguished for learning and eloquence. I do not recognize a Ciceronian who has to be driven from the imitation of Cicero by a scourge.

Bu.—St. Augustine then?

No.—He is like Cicero in that he makes his periods very long and involved. But he is not so clever in breaking up the extended structure of his oration into divisions nor has he Cicero's ready speech and felicity in handling subjects.

Bu.—Paulinus?

No.—He shows hardly a vestige of Cicero—commonplace in thoughts and words.

Bu.—St. Ambrose then.

No.—You cite a Roman orator, not a Ciceronian. He delights in clever allusions and general reflections, expresses himself only in aphorisms, abounds in rhythmical divisions and clauses and nicely balanced periods, has his own inimitable style but it is very different from Cicero's.

Bu.—At least acknowledge Pope Gregory I.

No.—I recognize in him a pious and sincere man. He is more like Cicero than St. Ambrose but his speech flows sluggishly and shows the influence of Isocrates, which is foreign to Cicero, for in his boyhood he had been so trained in the schools.

Bu.—Every one marvels at the eloquence of Pope Leo.

No.—His language is, I admit, rhythmical, clear and sensible, but not Ciceronian.

Bu.—What if I should suggest St. Bernard of Burgundy.

No.—I recognize in him a good man, which is a requisite for an orator, naturally disposed to refined and pleasing speech but so far from being a Ciceronian that you would scarcely gather from his writings that he had ever even read Cicero.

Bu.—Since you have rejected St. Bernard, I should not dare to propose to you Bede, Remi, Claudius, Hesychius, Anselm, Isidore.

No.—Do not mention those κολοζώτας[1] for their translations are miserable and their native speech worse. In them eloquence languished.

Bu.—I fear you will say *died* if I mention those who lived later. I shall omit therefore Alexander of Hales, Peter of Ghent, and innumerable writers of this calibre. I will suggest two κορυφαίους,[2] Bonaventure and Thomas.

No.—Bonaventure is fluent enough in his way; while Thomas is a true Aristotelian ἀπαθής,[3] aiming only to instruct the reader.

Bu.—That is true in investigations; but when he becomes rhetorician or poet you see the spirit of Cicero distinctly enough.

No.—Poet you say? Nowhere does he seem less eloquent than when he aims at oratorical fluency in the handling of the Eucharist. But come, to dismiss those scholastic theologians in whom you will seek in vain for any, much less Ciceronian, eloquence. Present others if you have them.

Bu.—Well, we will come back to another class of writers nearer to our own time. For several generations eloquence seems to have died out entirely, but not so long ago it began to come to life among the Italians, then later among our own people. And thus, the chief of the reflowering eloquence seems to have been the Italian, Francesco Petrarch, celebrated and great in his time, but now scarcely read—a man of burning genius, wide knowledge, and extraordinary eloquence.

No.—I admit it. And yet there are times when he halts in the use of Latin and his whole diction smacks of the rudeness of the preceding age. Moreover, who would call one a Ciceronian who did not even strive for the distinction?

---

[1] Mutilators.
[2] Eminent men.
[3] Without passion.

Bu.—There's no use then in suggesting Biondo and Boccaccio, who were inferior to Petrarch, both in eloquence and in the understanding of Latin. Nor even Giovanni Tortelli.

No.—No, indeed!

Bu.—He had a host of learned followers who eagerly set themselves to the imitation of Cicero. Do you consider any of them worthy of the name? Francesco Filelfo?

No.—Evidently he would be if he had pleased all as well as he pleased himself. He tried industriously to imitate Cicero but not very successfully. When he tried hardest, he failed most completely; for example, in his orations. Now in his letters there is some suggestion of Cicero. I would not have you think that I have meant to disparage these men. I recognize them as worthy of immortality and as having done great service to literature, but it is something divine to be a Ciceronian.

Bu.—[1]Leonardo Aretino seems to me a second Cicero.

No.—In ready speech and clearness he is much like Cicero, but he lacks Cicero's strength and some of his other virtues. He rarely gets a glimpse of pure Latinity. Aside from this, he is as learned as he is good.

Bu.—Guarino, I know well enough you would not allow, or Lapo, or Acciaiolo, or Antonio Beccaria, or Francesco Barbatius, or Antonio Tudertino, or Leonardus Justinianus, or Achille Bocchi, or others whose names do not occur to me, especially since most of them we know only through their translating from the Greek where originality, the chief part of eloquence, has no place.

No.—I scorn none of them yet I deem none worthy of the honor.

Bu.—I will present the Florentine, Poggio, a man of rather spirited style.

No.—He had natural ability enough but little training and sometimes his speech lacked purity, if we are to believe Lorenzo Valla.

Bu.—Then let us substitute Valla.

No.—He uses the purest idiom of all and is the most polished but he approaches nearer to the carefulness and subtlety of Quintilian than to the careless ease of Cicero.

---

[1]Leonordo Bruni.

Bu.—I consciously am passing over many whom I know you will not listen to and am proposing only the exceptional. If you confer the honor of this name upon any one at all, you will certainly grant it to Ermolao Barbaro the Great.

No.—You have introduced a truly great and divine man, but very unlike Cicero in style and more labored almost than Quintilian himself and Pliny whose eloquence the study of philosophy injured somewhat.

Bu.—What about Giovanni Pico della Mirandola?

No.—You mention an almost divine talent, an unbounded genius, but one whose zeal for language, philosophy and even theology has marred his eloquence.

Bu.—You know his namesake, Francesco?

No.—'Οὐδ' ἐγγύς,[1] as the saying is, too much a philosopher and theologian, otherwise a great man. But how does it happen that you count him among the Ciceronians, when in his dispute with Pietro Bembo, he denounced the devotees of Cicero?

Bu.—Granting that one can be too much of a theologian, you have praised him most highly.

No.—One can be for the gaining of this palm.

Bu.—The chances are that there is one, unless I am mistaken, to be found whom you will not reject—Angelo Politian. For Marsilio Ficino I do not dare to introduce.

No.—I confess that Angelo was of perfectly *angelic* mind, a rare miracle of nature in any field he has tried; but when compared to Cicero's style he is as nothing. His virtues are of a very different kind.

Bu.—Suppose I put into the list Codrus Urceo, George of Trebizonde, Theodore Gaza, John Lascaris, George Merula, Marcus Musurus, Marullo. I can almost guess your answer. You would bar from this contest the whole race of Greeks because you would say they hated your beloved Cicero. But no sentiment of anger, hate, or love should influence this election.

No.—Nor shall it. We must speak rather guardedly of John Lascaris, since he is still alive. He is a man of courteous manner, good breeding, and keen judgment. His epigrams are very clever. He might have been a promising candidate for Ciceronianism, if business of the state had not diverted his mind. Codrus Urelo had no skill in Latin nor culture. A man of the Epicurean

---

[1] Not near.

type, he troubled not himself about a prize which is as difficult
to obtain as it is uncommon. George of Trebizonde, I acknowledge, is a remarkably learned man who has done noble service
to letters, and yet Theodore Gaza is more finished. The one
has devoted himself to Cicero, the other to Aristotle; and no one
has made more elegant translations, whether from Greek into
Latin or Latin into Greek, than George of Trebizonde. When he
speaks his own tongue, however, two definite things annoy the
fastidious reader: his zeal for philosophy, in which he was absorbed; and that γνήσιον[1] of the Greek which is hard to unlearn.

Bu.—What hinders a Greek from mastering Latin, if a Briton
or a Frisian can? Especially when the Greek language, not only
in words but also in figures, has most affinity to the Latin?

No.—What the Britons and the Frisians have done I leave to
others. Affinity seems to me to stand in the way of purity.
More quickly will an Irishman speak pure Latin than a Frenchman or a Spaniard. More quickly will a Frenchman learn to
speak pure German than he will learn to speak Italian or Span-
ish. However, I shall proceed. George Merula is an Alexan-
drine. I do not know whether he is a Greek or not but his
Greek translations are so fine that he can be compared favorably
with many of the classical scholars. I have read a few things by
Marullo which would be tolerable if they contained less paganism.
Marcus Musurus I know better. He is a remarkably well in-
formed man, somewhat obscure and affected in his poetry, and
leaving nothing, so far as I know, in prose, except one or two
prefaces. I used to wonder how a Greek knew so much Latin.
He did little writing, because he was summoned to Rome by
Pope Leo to the office of archbishop and soon after died.

Bu.—You will accept Pomponio Leto then?

No.—Content with the elegance of Latin conversation he
learned nothing else.

Bu.—Well, Platina?

No.—He would have been a worthy historian if he had lighted
upon a happier theme. In his *optimus civis* and *Panegyricus* he
resembled Cicero but not enough to earn the name of Ciceronian.
In general, he was a learned man, versatile, and, I think, good.

Bu.—What of Filippo Beroaldo, the Elder? I see you shake
your head. I knew it.

---

[1]Accent.

7

No.—I will assent if you recommend him to me as a man of unusual merit in the realm of literature but if you demand that he be enrolled in the list of Ciceronians I must say no. Filippo Beroaldo, the Younger, stands a better chance, although he has made but small contribution to letters.

Bu.—In vain do I enumerate Giorgio Valla, Christophoro Landino, Mancinelli, Peter Marsus, Baptista Pius, Cornelio Vitelli, Nicolo Leoniceno and Leonico, Bartolommeo Scala, Paolo Cortesi, Pietro Crinito, Jacopo Antiquario.

No.—What a hodgepodge! Do not mention Mancinelli, Vitelli, and Marsi, when style is the subject for discussion. Baptista Pius tried for a style of his own. Scala in his own estimation was a Ciceronian but in that of Politian he had not even common sense, much less Latin scholarship. Paolo Cortesi I will discuss later. Pietro Crinito is a scholar yet he falls far short of being a Ciceronian. Leoniceno is a physician, not a rhetorician. Leonico ever busied in the sanctuaries of philosophy, especially in those of Plato, set himself to imitating the dialogues of Plato and Cicero and gained as much eloquence as we could expect from a philosopher; but he would not desire to be called a Ciceronian, I'm sure, for he is a man of rectitude as well as of profound learning.

Bu.—What of Domizio Calderino?

No.—He had a good start and would have stood a fair chance if dissipation at Rome and death had not cut him off in his youth.

Bu.—Next Scipio Carteromacho.

No.—I recognize in him a man without ostentation, and versed in both Latin and Greek, but from his writings it does not appear that he aimed at Ciceronian eloquence.

Bu.—You will not reject, I suppose, Girolamo Donato, the noble Venetian?

No.—His letters—about the only thing of his we have—show that he could have accomplished anything he turned his mind to but politics distracted him from literary work.

Bu.—Antonio Sabellicus?

No.—I acknowledge he has natural ability and some skill in speaking. And he uses his rhetoric not unsuccessfully at times. He has done brilliant work in that kind of history which calls for his particular style.

Bu.—Thus far the host of dead. Now we ought, as they say, to remember the living, of whom perhaps you will hesitate to say what you think.

No.—Not at all, since I admit that this measure of praise has been the good fortune of practically no one up to the present time

Bu.—You know Paolo Aemilio?

No.—The man's profound learning, painstaking care, purity of life, and entire trustworthiness in history, I greatly admire. Ciceronian style he neither aimed at nor has.

Bu.—I bring Battista Egnazio.

No.—You have mentioned a man as honest and blameless as he is learned and eloquent but to whom the votes of the doctors deny the honor of the Ciceronian name. He preferred to speak learnedly rather than in Ciceronian style and he gained what he wished.

Bu.—See, I bring to you Paolo Bombasio.

No.—Indeed I admire Paolo Bombasio, a man of absolutely golden heart, the best friend in the world; but, on account of his health, he did not indulge much in writing. Of sensitive nature, he was soon offended at the wicked contentions of mean rivals. He taught Greek at Bologna for a salary; devoted himself to the business of the state; and, when at length summoned to Rome, he preferred to increase his estate rather than to grow old in letters.

Bu.—Perhaps you will be more favorable to younger men. What do you think of Andria Alciati?

No.—I will give you the opinion of scholars who knew the man better than I. The virtues which Cicero divided between Quintus Scaevola and Marcus Crassus, the one of whom he called the most legal minded of orators and the other the most eloquent of lawyers, both in this one man are said to meet. His power of eloquence we have seen in the preface of Cornelius Tacitus. For in the *Annotations* he meant to teach, not to speak as an orator.

Bu.—We have omitted few Italians, I suppose, worthy of mentioning. But Jerome Aleander, who was recently a favorite of Clement VII and Archbishop of Brundusium, ought not to be overlooked.

No.—His ability is not sufficiently clear from what he has written; for few of his things have been published and in these par-

ticular ones he does not seem to have striven for Ciceronianism.
For a long time business of state turned him in a different direction and, though he was skilled in both Latin and Greek, he was
absolutely unworthy the honor because a slave to business.

Bu.—Indeed I think Albert, Prince of Carpi, approached nearer
to Ciceronian phrase than Aleander. He has written nothing, so
far as I know, except a single book, or, if you prefer, a lengthy
letter in answer to Erasmus, and even of this some declare posi-
tively that he is not the author.

No.—Whatever his merits, he approaches Cicero just so far
as one may who has been trained from his youth in theology and
philosophy.

Bu.—You see how many writers of most celebrated name I
have called to mind, Nosoponus, no one of whom you admit to
have attained the dignity of a Ciceronian. Perchance some
escape me. Suggest if you know any, Hypologus.

Hyp.—The two Cælii, Rhodiginus and Calcagini you have intentionally omitted?

Bu.—Certainly not intentionally.

No.—Rhodiginus was a good man and widely read but not to
be entered in the contest of eloquence at all; Calcagini was not
only superior in eloquence but also in learning, of elegant and
ornate style, but smacking somewhat of scholastic philosophy
which does not hinder him from being numbered among the eloquent but bars him from the Ciceronians.

Bu.—A very few I pass by consciously, to the mention of
whom our discussion will naturally bring us around at a more
fitting time. Meantime, if you please, let us go across for a
little while into France, always most flourishing in letters, to
bring up for consideration at least the principal ones who have
recently won a reputation for eloquence through their writings.
Robert Gaguin not so very long ago was very popular, more
however, on account of his speeches than his writings.

No.—Yes, but in his own age. Now he would hardly be
counted a Latin scholar.

Bu.—What if I should introduce the two brothers Ferdinand?

No.—I would not allow it.

Bu.—Jouvenneaux Gui?

No.—Much less.

Bu.—Jodocus Badius?

No.—More quickly I should admit him into the contest than Apuleius, for his attempts have not been fruitless; he has ability and skill and would have attained greater success if domestic cares and avarice had not interrupted the leisure conducive to the Muses and necessary for an aspirant to this honor.

Bu.—Perhaps the honor of this title you will grant to Guillaume Budé, the glory of France.

No.—Why should I grant what he does not strive for and would not recognize if I should? Still, he deserves admiration in other respects for his great and varying gifts.

Bu.—Jacob Faber is very highly esteemed.

No.—A good man and a scholar but one who preferred to speak in the language of theology rather than in that of Cicero.

Bu.—Jean Pins perchance you will take.

No.—He might have been numbered among the competitors if the stress of business and ecclesiastical office had not turned him away from his studies. Once indeed at Bologna he demonstrated his power when he made offerings to the Muses. Now, I hear, he has been made a bishop and what increase of eloquence has come to him I do not know. Perchance he has gained more learning than honorable employment.

Bu.—Do you recognize Nicolas Bérauld?

No.—I recognize that he is not unlike Pins in spontaneity but he has never directed his strength to Ciceronian style. He is more successful in speaking than in writing. I divine perfectly well his abilities but he is rather inclined to be lazy.

Bu.—Franciscus Deloinus I should not hesitate to suggest, if he could have shown himself as great in oration or essay as in letters written extemporaneously to friends. It would surely have seemed strange if he had wasted almost his whole life *in Accursiis, Bartholis, ac Baldis,* and if in his old age he had fortunately grown young again in more polite letters. Death recently has called him away; timely for himself because he was an old man, but prematurely for letters because he seemed destined to their elevation and adornment. If Lazare de Baif, who by a single little essay on clothes won great renown and raised the highest hopes, only had gone on as he began! Although fitted for teaching, he preferred to be witty as it seems, and a representative of the Attic school rather than a Ciceronian.

Bu.—There occurs to me at this moment a pair, by no means,
I fancy, to be scorned. You know Claude Chansonnette of
Metz, and Cornelius Scepper?

No.—Both, intimately. Chansonnette is of a playful turn of
mind, sings most sweetly any theme whatever, especially in prose;
in poetry I do not know his ability. Not unsuccessfully does he
imitate Cicero. The fluency, perspicuity, wealth of language, and
wit of Cicero he has almost attained, and though for a long time
he has been playing a vivacious role in the legations of princes,
in spite of the fact that this task requires the deepest quiet, he
has conquered himself, just as if he took all the Muses as his
companions with him when flitting over land and sea. He has
this remarkable distinction, viz., that he has combined eloquence
with knowledge of law and philosophy. Scepperus in addition
to skill in every department of learning weaves with equal facility
poetry and prose even though he now for a long time has been
taking active part in politics.

Bu.—What do you think of Ruel?

No.—That which is worthy of a man most skilled in medical
lore and most religiously faithful in translating Greek authors.
This kind of a reputation he preferred to being called a Ciceronian.

Bu.—But where must I place Peter Mosellanus of Treves,
among the Germans or the French?

No.—That has nothing to do, surely, with our present discussion.

Bu.—Among the Ciceronians?

No.—I admire his scholarship, equal in Latin and Greek, his
practical knowledge, his pure and unalloyed genius, his untiring
care, his lively, figurative, and clear diction. Much would have
been expected of him if he had not died in his youth, when just
entering the contest for this honor, causing sorrow to all scholars and a great loss to letters.

Bu.—From France then, if you please, let us turn to England,
the fortunate nurse of geniuses. But hold, I had almost forgotten German Brixius. You would not ignore a man equally
skilled in Latin and Greek, in poetry and prose, and successful
in Latin translations of Greek. Will you then class Brixius
among Ciceronians?

No.—Although he is still in the heat of the race and has attained fluency and clearness, yet he is unlike Cicero in some things, but in such things that he may have hope, if, as at present, he goes on devoting himself wholly to this study. Meantime, I like to applaud him because he is running zealously.

Bu.—Now then into England; and, since she has so many candidates, I will name only those who have sought fame through their writings. If I cite William Grocyn, you will say that there is nothing extant of his except a single letter, very carefully elaborated, clever, and in good Latin. Fitted for epistolary cleverness, he loved brevity and propriety; you would call him a representative of the Attic School in this surely, for he aimed at nothing else and could not endure Cicero's fulness of expression. He was laconic not only in writing but also in speaking. Therefore I shall not urge his claims. But I do not hesitate to propose Thomas Linacre.

No.—I know him as a man of excellent training but so disposed toward Cicero that, if he could have been like either he pleased, he would have preferred Quintilian to Cicero. Thus, you see, he was not much more kindly disposed toward Cicero than the common run of Greeks are. Urbanity he never strives for; he surpasses an Attic in the repression of his feelings; brevity and elegance he loves, and he is extremely didactic. He studiously copies Aristotle and Quintilian. You may attribute him as much praise as you wish but he cannot be called a Ciceronian for he has studied to be unlike Cicero.

Bu.—There is Richard Pace.

No.—He indeed could have been counted among the candidates for Ciceronian eloquence, if the speed of extemporaneous writing had not been too alluring and if the business of popes and kings had not distracted him in his youth and almost buried him in worldly cares.

Bu.—I will leave England when I have mentioned Thomas More.

No.—A most fortunate genius. I confess there is nothing he could not have accomplished if he had devoted himself wholly to letters. But in his boyhood scarcely a trace of the better literature had crossed into England. Then the authority of his parents compelled him to learn English Law, the farthest possible from literature; next he was exercised in pleading cases, then called to the duties of the state. With difficulty he could at odd hours turn his attention to the study of oratory. Finally he was dragged into Court and immersed in the business of the King and the Kingdom where he could love study but not cultivate it. Though the style he gained tended rather to Isocratic rhythm and logical subtlety than to the outpouring river of Ciceronian eloquence, yet he is not inferior at all in culture to Cicero. Furthermore, you recognize a poet even in his prose for in his youth he spent much time in writing poetry.

Bu.—Then let us leave England for I will not mention William Latimer or Reginald Pole—one of whom, a pious man, preferred to be proficient in theology rather than in the eloquence of Cicero, and the other, though a very great admirer and not a bad imitator of Cicero, has not cared to publish anything over his own name but has shown his ability in private letters. In other lines, England has innumerable youths of the highest hopes. We are, however, playing the part of the censor, not the soothsayer. Yet what wonder that youth flowers there where the King himself not only encourages talent by prizes but also spurs it on by his example, already having testified in two pamphlets his love of piety and shown his genius and his eloquence.

No.—I have admired those essays very much and they are not so different from Cicero except that the theme and royal dignity seem to require their own peculiar style.

Bu.—What then remains except to sail over to Holland?

No.—First to Scotland, I vote.

Bu.—I should not care, if I thought there was any one there whom you would consider. I'd rather go to Denmark for she has given to us Saxo Grammaticus who wrote a splendid history of that people.

No.—I admire so much his lively and burning genius, his rapid, flowing speech, his wonderful wealth of words, his numerous aphorisms, his wonderful variety of figures that I cannot wonder enough where a Dane of that age got so great power of eloquence; yet you will find scarcely a trace of Cicero in him.

Bu.—Now to Holland.

No.—No, to Zeland first, lest you slight some one.

Bu.—That land too has produced skillful minds but most of them are buried in luxury. Thence if you will I shall bring Adrian van Barland, in whose writings you can recognize the purity and ease of Cicero.

No.—He approximates Cicero, to be sure, in those qualities, but not in all.

Bu.—From Zeland it is an easy journey to Holland, prolific parent of native genius; but no honor is paid there to eloquence and pleasures do not easily allow talent to mature. From there I will bring Erasmus of Rotterdam, if you will allow.

No.—You profess to speak of writers. I do not call him a writer, much less a Ciceronian.

Bu.—What do I hear? Anyway he was counted among the πολυγράφοι[1]

No.—Yes, if a πολυγράφος is one who smears a great quantity of paper with ink. It is a different thing to write in the sense in which we are using the term, and writers make up a different class. Otherwise those who make money by transcribing books with the hand might be called writers, though scholars prefer to call them scribes. But that is writing in my mind which brings fruit from the field. Reading corresponds to the fertilizing; digesting and correcting corresponds to the harrowing, digging, trenching, pruning, pulling out of tares, and the rest of the work without which neither the seed will sprout nor, after sprouting, grow.

Bu.—What then is your opinion of Erasmus?

No.—He degrades and hurries everything; he does not give natural birth to his creations; sometimes he writes a whole volume at one sitting; nor can he ever have patience to read over even once what he has written; and he does nothing but write, notwithstanding the fact that not till after long reading should one come to writing and then but seldom. What of the fact too that he not even tries for Ciceronian style but uses theological words and sometimes even vulgarisms?

Bu.—William Gaudanus was terser.

No.—Brief as an Attic in his letters, good in poetry, but— O accursed ease! how much of fine natural ability do you' either spoil or utterly destroy!

Bu.—You know Gilles de Delft?

No.—A man of wide learning, not a bad versifier, if he had added strength to facility.

Bu.—Martin Dorpius died but recently.

---

[1] Writers of many books.

No.—Fruitful, versatile, and inclined to elegance, but preferring to be led by others' counsels. Finally, theology separated him from the Muses.

Bu.—What do you think of Jacob Ceratinus?

No.—He gave promise but is far from a Ciceronian.

Bu.—Thence then, if you please, let us journey together into Friesland. For that country produces minds absolutely white, as the saying goes. But Como is ill suited to the Muses. Therefore I shall omit the Langes, and the Canters; Rodolph Agricola alone is a sufficient representative.

No.—I recognize in him a man of divine heart, of profound learning, of no common style, genuine, strong, painstaking, orderly, but smacking somewhat of Quintilian in style and of Isocrates in structure, yet more sublime than either, also more fluent and clearer than Quintilian. He accomplished his aim and I do not doubt that he could have portrayed Cicero if he had wished. And yet there were certain other things that stood in the way of his attaining this highest reputation—the misfortune of place and time, for in his day and country practically no honor at all was paid to polite letters and the national life was extravagant. In Italy he could have excelled but he preferred Germany.

Bu.—Hayo Hermanus is of the same race.

No.—A young man of divine talent; yet there is extant no specimen of his power except some letters, unrivalled in purity, healthy tone, and sweetness. He perchance would have gained the palm if he had been as industrious as he was gifted.

Bu.—I vote that we cross to Westphalia, which has given us Alexander von Heck.

No.—Yes, you mention one who is learned, pure, and eloquent but who has accomplished nothing great because of his contempt for fame.

Bu.—Westphalia has given us Hermann von dem Busche also.

No.—In poetry successful, in prose showing great strength of mind, wide reading, keen judgment, plenty of force; but his style is more like Quintilian than Cicero.

Bu.—Conrad Goclenius, I presume, you do not know.

No.—Do you mean him who in Brabant has for so long adorned not only the college *Busleidianus*—called by some *Trilingue*—but also that whole Academy, and who was otherwise most distinguished?

Bu.—That very one.

No.—I know him Καὶ οἴκοθεν·[1]

Bu.—Do you find any deficiency in him whereby he may not be counted among the Ciceronians?

No.—I think that that mind could accomplish whatever it seriously wished but he prefers to take life easy rather than to be voluminous.

Hyp.—I know one point in which he is very unlike Cicero.

Bu.—What is that?

Hyp.—We picture Cicero with a long and slender neck. Goclenius had a beautifully plump one, and so short that the chin almost touched his breast.

Bu.—We are not discussing his neck but his pen. Suppose, however, we leave Westphalia. Saxony has young men of hope and extraordinary promise among whom Christophorus Carlebitzius is very distinguished on account of the services of his ancestors to the state, and even more on account of his own exemplary character and literary work; but I will not weary you with the enumeration of men whose genius is still growing, who, so to speak, are still in the blade. I will proceed to the other Germans, chief among whom was Reuchlin.

No.—A great man, but his speech is redolent of his age which was still somewhat rough and unpolished. In the same class are Jacob Wimpheling and others whose works contributed not a little to the literature of Germany. And yet he, in a certain way, had his second youth in his grandson, Jacob Spiegel.

Bu.—Then you recognize Philip Melancthon as a pupil of Reuchlin?

No.—Most successful would he have been if he had devoted himself wholly to the Muses. As it was he exerted himself but little and, content with the gifts of nature, he showed little practice or care in his writing and it may be his health would have failed him if he had tried. He seems naturally fitted for extemporaneous speaking but absorbed in other things he seems to have largely given up the study of oratory.

Bu.—Then let me bring to you Ulrich von Hutten.

No.—Splendor and wealth enough he shows in prose, more in verse; but he was far from being the image of Cicero.

---

[1] Intimately.

Bu.—Bilibaldus I ought to have mentioned before, for under his leadership eloquence first began to flourish in Germany, which he illuminated by the purity of his character and the splendor of his fortune.

No.—I do not know whether he aspires, surely he has not attained and his native ability is not so much in the way as business of state and poor health, though no one is more worthy of the best. Yet writing so happily without preparation shows how much he might do if he could put his strength to it.

Bu.—All Germany gives the highest praise to Ulric Zazius.

No.—Yet less than he merited, for besides an exact knowledge of the law, which is his profession, he has a certain very happy faculty of speaking and writing even extemporaneously so that you might say his speech flows out from some rich spring in good, well-chosen words and sentences unceasingly; and there is in his writings a youthful alacrity, and, if I may use the term, vivacity which would make you say that it is not the work of an old man you are reading. Yet, withal, he imitates Politian more nearly than Cicero.

Bu.—Well, from a spot near by I will bring Bruno Amerbach, of Augst than whom nature has never fashioned any more promising.

No.—As far as one may know from a taste, he would have been great if death had not snatched him away prematurely from his studies.

Bu.—Henricus Glareanus, the Swiss, you know?

No.—He preferred to spend his time on philosophy and mathematics rather than to imitate Ciceronian phrase, which hardly fits the subtleties of mathematicians.

Bu.—There is one left whom if you do not accept we shall go across into Pannonia.

No.—Who?

Bu.—Ursinus Velius.

No.—Successful in poetry but not in prose. He has plenty of feeling and culture; but when the history which he is said to be writing on the exploits of King Ferdinand of Pannonia and Bohemia is published we can decide more definitely.

Bu.—I am certain he will respond with vigor and eloquence to the renown of his chief and his great deeds. Mention of him has brought us into Pannonia, where I know no one except Jacob

Piso, a zealous candidate for Ciceronian eloquence, who was first snatched away from us by the Court, then by misfortune, and recently by death itself.

No.—I heard and was much grieved.

Bu.—And Sarmatia has men whom you could not despise, but I shall mention none except those who by publishing have given proof of themselves. Chief among these is Bishop Andreas Critius, who surely has wit at command, as the saying goes, who composes verses happily, even more happily prose, who writes extemporaneously with ease and makes conversation pleasing by his perpetual humor.

No.—I have tasted some little bits of his which surely raise in me high hopes, if he is not compelled to give up the leisure needed for the pursuit of the Muses because of embassies of State and Church.

Bu.—Spain who has begun to flower again and to vie with her early glory has very many learned and eloquent men and a few who have become famous through their writings, among whom is Antonio de Lebrixa, a man of wide knowledge. But the mention of him you would not allow in the catalogue of Ciceronians.

No.—You have guessed rightly.

Bu.—Not even Lopes, I think, or Sanchez.

No.—One is a theologian and did not strive for this reputation, the other is much less successful in eulogy than in panegyric, neither the one nor the other is a Ciceronian.

Bu.—I wonder if you will reject John Louis Vives.

No.—Indeed I find lacking in him neither talent, learning, nor memory; he has a ready store of thoughts and words; he was a little too stilted in the beginning, but he grows more eloquent daily; and if neither life nor zeal fail there is hope that he will be numbered among the Ciceronians. There are those however whose attempts at writing come out as the gifts of Mandrabulus. He excels himself daily. He has a versatile mind and thus is fitted especially for public speaking. Yet some of the virtues of Cicero he has not attained, particularly that of pleasing speech and flexibility.

Bu.—Also I know some learned Portuguese who have given public proof of their genius. But I have direct knowledge of none of them except a certain Hermicus, who is successful at epigram, quick and facile in prose, and of very skillful wit in prattling; and Genesius, who recently showed great hope of himself through his pamphlet published at Rome.

See how many lands we have traversed seeking a single Ciceronian, Nosoponus; and not one has been found whom you deem worthy of the honor of the name of your lover! How many ancients we have called to mind, how many of later ages, how many of the age preceding our own, how many of our own contemporaries! Some of them, I grant, a fastidious censor would not accept; but many of them have ornamented, illuminated, and ennobled their age, country, church, and literature by their learning and eloquence; and, up to the present point, we have found no Ciceronian. What remains for us but to go to the Islands of the Blessed for the purpose of seeking there one to whom we may give this name?

With more content we suffer a misfortune common to all. A Spaniard does not grieve if he has not yellow hair, nor an Indian because he is of sallow complexion, nor an Ethiopian because he is black and his nose is flat. Then why do you torture your mind and chafe because you are not a Ciceronian? This may be an ill; but, if it is, can you not bear an ill common to you and such men as we have mentioned?

No.—But Christophe de Longueil, a native of Brabant and educated among the French, attained the reputation. To him alone on this side the Alps the Italians granted this palm; all others they cast aside as barbarians.

Bu.—To be sure De Longueil won highest praise but he won it at too great a price. Long he tortured himself and finally died in the midst of his struggle, causing no small loss to letters to which he would have been in his lifetime of greater use if he had not turned his mind and all his strength of genius to the desire of an empty name. And yet he did not devote himself entirely to Cicero but read every kind of author, studied carefully all the liberal arts, and had a practical knowledge of law besides. Nor was he content to follow in the footsteps of Cicero, but was seemingly very clever in invention, and fertile, skillful, and happy in argument, never failing to show proof of a genius worthy of admiration. It amounts to nothing that these apes of Cicero throw De Longueil in our teeth; he would have been great for his other gifts, even if he had not been a Ciceronian; and this very ambition for an empty title almost destroyed the fruit of his studies and finally cost him his life. Still he was very different from Cicero for he lacked the opportunity of exercising that wonderful eloquence which Cicero exhibited in grave and serious cases in court.

De Longueil published letters, which, though elegant and cleverly wrought, were, I confess, many of them on very trivial subjects and many more were as far-fetched as those of Pliny the Younger. Such products I think ought not to be ranked as letters. Tell me what characteristics of a letter have the *Epistolae* of Seneca except the name? But you say that in Cicero's letters nothing is far-fetched. Either he writes on weighty and serious business as he would speak in public, or he talks with absent friends on familiar themes or about literary pursuits as friends do in ordinary conversation. What of the fact that he did not publish his letters and that he seems to have written some more carelessly than he was accustomed to talk? Why did a great part of those which Tiro, the freedman, collected perish? I think they would not have perished if scholars had judged them worthy of immortality. In the first place then, Cicero's simplicity and charm of unaffected speech; in the second place, his truthfulness is lacking in most of the letters of De Longueil. And inasmuch as neither the fortune nor the business of De Longueil was the same as Cicero's, his imitation lacks fitness and life. To illustrate—Cicero, when a senator and of consular rank, writes to his peers what the generals are doing in the provinces, how the legions are drawn up, points out the dangers, and prophesies the outcome; De Longueil, in imitation of Cicero, writes similar things to learned friends in times of peace and shows anxiety about the outcome of affairs. Do not his efforts fail? Consider that in the privacy of his library he committed to writing most idle rumors such as commonly float about, unworthy to be mentioned even in the conversation of sensible men.

But you say that in the two orations which he left, as if delivered in the Capitol, he has given us Cicero. These, I confess, I have read not only with great admiration but also with great delight; for they caused me to feel far more than ever before the genius of the man. So much so that, though I had formed a fine opinion of him, he far surpassed my expectation; for he seems to have brought forth in these

orations whatever power he had of his own and what he had
drunk from the orations of Cicero. Yet these speeches which
were worked on for so many years, revised so many times, so
many times subjected to the censorship of critics,—how little
have they of Cicero! No fault indeed of De Longueil, but of
the times. Cicero spoke in perfect keeping with his times, not
so De Longueil; for at Rome today there are neither the Conscript Fathers, nor the Senate, nor the authority of the people,
nor the votes of the tribes, nor the regular magistrates, nor the
laws, nor the comitia, nor legal procedure, nor provinces, nor
towns, nor allies, nor citizens,—and Rome, there is no Rome, for
there is nothing but ruin and rubbish, scars and tracks of old-
time calamity. Take away the pope, the cardinals, the bishops,
the curia and its officials, the embassadors, the churches, colleges
and abbeys, and the rabble—a part of whom live on trafficking
and the other part are such as have drifted thither seeking liberty
or fortune—and what will Rome be? You answer that the
authority of the Popes handed down by Christ is grander than
was formerly the rule of the Senate and the Roman People, or
even, if you please, of Octavius Caesar. Suppose it is, only
acknowledge that the kind of rule is different. Then you see
that the same language will not fit, if we decide that it is Ciceronian to fit the language to the present theme. But that celebrated youth fitted his speech to the emotions of men who dream
of ancient Rome, *rerum dominam gentemque togatam*, just as the
Jews dream of their Moses and the temple at Jerusalem. Young
Christophe was great, I say, not on account of office, or exploits,
or for any other reason except for his own ability, which I think
is much finer than if he had ruled a kingdom.

This however, has nothing to do with Cicero. Back to the case.
A dispute arose between him and a certain Italian youth, who I
suppose, was primed to protect Ciceronian eloquence against the
barbarians. And there is, I hear, now a sort of society at Rome
of such men who have more learning than piety, who are called
scholars and are held in high esteem by many. Through the
influence of these idlers the dispute kindled into fires of partisan-
ship on both sides, for Rome seeks material for pleasure from
every source. As time went on the actions of Luther injured
De Longueil; for, on account of Luther, whatever had to do
with Germany, in fact any one on this side the Alps, was in bad

repute at Rome. Some few, more fair-minded than the others, thought it proper to bestow upon De Longueil the title of Roman citizen, as a mark of honor, notwithstanding the fact that he was a barbarian by birth—they still use words of this kind as if the whole face of the world had not changed—because of the admirable elegance of his language. In ancient days this was done and it was a gift as useful as it was honorable. But now, what is it to be Roman citizen? Indeed something less than to be a citizen of Basle. Out of this grew the rivalry of the youth and his coterie against the barbarian De Longueil. The society of idlers sought satisfaction by having De Longueil plead his case in the Capitol (for so they called the hall in which plays are accustomed to be performed by the boys for the sake of practice). An upstart of a youth was suborned to present the indictment, which had been drawn up by some one else and had been memorized. The headings of the indictment were:—first, Christophe de Longueil, once in his boyhood, when, for the sake of testing his strength, he was praising the country where he was then living, had dared to compare France favorably with Italy; second, he had praised the barbarians, Erasmus and Budé; third, incited and delegated by them he had come into Italy to carry back to the barbarians all the best books so that thus they might vie with the Italians for the chief place of learning; and finally, on the ground that he was an uncivilized man and of obscure family he did not seem worthy of so great an honor as to be called a Roman. Here is a theme on which you may test the powers of Ciceronian eloquence. De Longueil treated with utmost seriousness this plainly ridiculous charge, manifesting a truly wonderful pomp of words, a great show of talent, the greatest vehemence, at times much urbanity, using the age of Cicero just as the author of "The Battle of Frogs and Mice" made use, in sport, of the Homeric Iliad, fitting to frogs and mice and equally ridiculous things the splendid words and deeds of gods, goddesses, and heroes. He exaggerated the danger of his position, picturing armed cohorts and bands of gladiators by whom the authority of the Senate and the free action of the law had been hindered. He set before them in fancy early Rome, the Queen of the World, and Romulus with his *Quirites* as her guard and protector; then the Common People and the ruling Senate, the people divided into classes and tribes, the Praetorian

8

right, the veto of the Tribunes; he pictured provinces, colonies
towns, allies of the Seven-hilled City; he quoted a decree of the
Senate; he cited laws:—I marvel that he did not remember the
water-clocks, nine of which I think are allowed to the defendant
Next the emotions were called into play; the old statesmen o'
the Roman Republic were appealed to and summoned forth from
their tombs. What was not done? The proceeding was exceed
ingly humorous.

I, for my part, confess it would be a good thing if our
young men were trained thus in the schools of declamation
in spite of the fact that Quintilian teaches that the prac
tice of declamation should approach as nearly as possible to the
real pleading—no doubt because some like to seek themes from
the stories of poets which are neither real nor probable; and
because, though the preparatory exercises bear valuable frui
even when the subject is taken from history and the words and
thoughts are made to suit the conditions of other times, yet the
youth will be better instructed to plead a real case if he handles
an investigation involved in the circumstances of the presen
day. For example, these would be more useful subjects: whether
it would profit the state for princes to give their daughters and
sisters in marriage to distant regions; whether it would be to the
advantage of Christian piety for the leading churchmen to be
burdened with secular rule; whether a young man can gain a
better education by wide reading than by traveling through dis
tant lands; or whether it is profitable for a boy, elected to rule
by choice of the people or by birth, to spend much time on letter
and the liberal arts.

Since De Longueil's theme was not taken from history, how
could it be made consistent with its time by fictitious assump
tion? and since, on the other hand, it was not of such a
kind that it could be consistent with its own time and charac
ters, how could he imitate Cicero exactly, who, when the arm
of Antony had been defeated, laying aside the fear of death
spoke freely before the Senate and the Roman People? The dis
tinguished youth, in spite of these difficulties, conducted the cas
with so much zeal and skill that I know of no one today ever
among the Italians, with due respect to all I say it, who could
do as well. Thus you see I have no desire to detract from the
glory of De Longueil, for such genius I should have to admir

even if found in an enemy. What I have said has only this in view that I may keep youthful students from superstitiously torturing themselves by striving after the likeness of Cicero to such an extent that they are turned away from more useful and necessary studies by the effort. You have the case before you, Nosoponus, the orations are extant to refute me if I have misrepresented anything. Now I should like to have you explain to me whether it is worth while for brilliant minds to spend so much time and trouble on these displays, to say nothing of killing themselves by such anxieties. How much more use De Longueil would have been to the Christian religion, to letters, and to his fatherland, if the nights he spent on these ridiculous indictments he had spent on serious subjects!

No.—Indeed, I am sorry for De Longueil and I have practically nothing to answer.

Bu.—Besides, he bears witness that he has written five orations in praise of Rome. O labor beautifully spent! How much better if he had sought to kindle that state and those men who professed belles-lettres there to the adoration of Christ and the love of piety by a few carefully wrought orations! You understand, Nosoponus, what I mean. And, pray tell me for whom so much labor was spent. For the Senate? The Senate, if there is any at Rome, does not know Latin. For the people? So far are they from being captivated by Ciceronian language that they speak a barbarian tongue. So farewell to these ostentatious displays!

He enters into a serious and weighty case against Martin Luther. In this can he be a Ciceronian when he is discussing things of which Cicero knew absolutely nothing! He cannot, for /the oration cannot be perfectly Ciceronian which does not accord with the age, the characters, and the circumstances./ He could assail in a fashion truly Ciceronian, but when it comes to the enumeration of the charges Cicero's phraseology would be rather obscure and hardly understood by those who held the tenets of Luther. Here the case requires the utmost clearness of expression, if he wishes to be a Ciceronian. Furthermore, from the way he sets forth the facts, it would not be difficult to guess what he would have been in refuting the doctrines of his adversary and in establishing his own. He carefully avoids the words of our religion, never using the word, *fides* (faith), but substituting in its place, *persuasio* (conviction), and many others which we have spoken of before. Yet time and again he uses the name of Christian, inadvertently, I presume, for this word never, occurred in the books of Cicero. Withal, there was much in the speech very praiseworthy; and the greatest fault was that he was so anxious to be a Ciceronian that he preferred to fit his language to Cicero rather than to the case.

No.—And yet it is wonderful how much at the present time some Italians praise these orations.

Bu.—I confess that they praise them, but they read others. How many more thumb the pages of the popular trifles of the [1]Dutch orator which are called the *Colloquia* than the writings of De Longueil however carefully wrought, however finished, however Ciceronian, or to put it in Greek better, κεκροτημένα ![2] What is the reason? Why, I say, unless because in the latter the subject itself holds and attracts the reader, no matter in what style it is handled; while over the former the reader sleeps and snores because they are lifeless and artificial? Usefulness recommends even mediocre eloquence. That which merely furnishes amusement cannot continue to please, especially if those who are reading have the end in view not only to speak with greater polish but to live better. In fine, those who inflamed this youth to the striving after Ciceronianism did not deserve the highest reward either from him or from the literary world. But of De Longueil perchance too much.

No.—You have hurried past Jacob Sadolet and Pietro Bembo with reason, I suppose.

Bu.—Yes, for I was not willing to mix excellent men and rare examples of their time with the mob. None of Pietro Bembo's work is extant that I know of except some letters in which I admire the very clear, sane, and I may say Attic style of speaking, as well as the honesty, gentleness, and singular purity of genius, reflected in the language as in a mirror. In nothing do I think De Longueil more fortunate or more adorned than in the friendship of such men. Jacob Sadolet in almost all respects equals Bembo; but he does not strive so much, in that most elegant commentary which he published on the fiftieth psalm, to be considered a Ciceronian that he fails to preserve the charm of his

[1] Erasmus himself
[2] Applauded.

character, for he was Bishop of Carpentras and had full regard
for his theme. And he used some ecclesiastical words in his letters
too. What then? Did he not speak in Ciceronian style? No,
or rather yes; for he spoke as Cicero would probably have spoken
of the same things if he had lived at that time,—that is, of
Christian themes in Christian language. Ciceronians of this kind
I can endure, who, gifted with the highest genius, finished with
every kind of training, of singular judgment and wisdom, cannot
but use the best language whether they have as examples Cicero
alone, or a few superior men, or all the scholars.

No.—The scholars think very well of Battista Casellius.

Bu.—The oration *De Lege Agraria* which was published a little
while before his death shows that he strove for the formal part
of the Ciceronian style with all his might, and that in this he
succeeded very well for there was a very high degree of illustration, brilliance of language, and persuasion. For the rest, his
deficiency is great if you compare him with Cicero.

No.—Surely all unanimously praise Pontano. The votes of
scholars grant to him the palm of Ciceronian style.

Bu.—I am not so stupid nor so envious as not to confess
that Pontano was of the first rank in many excellent gifts of
genius. And he captivates me too with the quiet flow of his
style; he charms my ear by a lovely tinkling of sweet sounding
words; and he overpowers me with a kind of splendor and ma-
jestic dignity of style.

No.—What hinders then your acknowledging him to be a
Ciceronian?

Bu.—What I have said does not make him a Ciceronian. I
have read a few of his works. He handles secular subjects and
what may be called commonplaces, such as fortitude, obedience,
excellence, which shine most easily and of themselves furnish an
abundance of maxims, in a way that you could scarcely tell
whether he were a Christian or not. Thus he manages his pen
in the pamphlet *De Principe*. I cannot remember what else I
have read of his except some dialogues modelled after Lucian.
But I do not recognize in him a Ciceronian unless he is a Ciceronian who handles modern life with Ciceronian felicity. In
epigrams he would have won more praise if he had shunned obscenity, which is not entirely lacking in his *Dialogi* either. In
Meteora and *Urania* he found material that easily became bril-

liant, and handled a happy theme in a happy way, using at times the vocabulary of the Christians. In his other works I find at times propriety and fitness and that pungency which lingers in the mind after one of Cicero's works is laid aside. Certainly, according to that law which you have laid down to us, he will not be a Ciceronian in whose writings I could show six hundred words not in Cicero. Finally, think how little Pontano is read, though he is one of the most prominent writers.

No.—Accius Syncerus, who succeeded Pontano, described the birth of the Virgin Mother in a wonderfully clever poem which was applauded beyond measure in the theater at Rome.

Bu.—The breviaries (for so they call them today) of Leo and Clement testify abundantly to this. Then a preface was added of Cardinal Aegedius, not to mention others, and it had reason to be pleasing. Indeed I read both books with delight. He wrote eclogues on fishing too. Who would not admire such talent in a noble youth? He must be placed before Pontano because he was not ashamed to write on a sacred theme and because he treated it neither in a sleepy nor in a disagreeable fashion, but he would have deserved more praise if he had treated his sacred subject somewhat more reverently. Indeed Battista Mantuano could excel him. What was the use of his invoking so many times in a sacred poem the Muses and Phoebus? of his painting the Virgin intent upon the verses of the Muses? of introducing Proteus foretelling Christ? and peopling the whole world with nymphs, hamadryads, and neriads? How harsh this verse sounds to Christian ears which, if I mistake not, is spoken to the Virgin Mary: *Tuque adeo spes fida hominum, spes fida Deorum!*[1] Of course *Deorum* for the sake of the meter was put in place of *Divorum*. Among so many virtues his frequent elisions count for little, but they mar the smoothness. To be brief: if you should cite this poem as a typical work of a youth studying to write poetry, I should think it good; but if as a poem written by a serious man on the subject of piety, I should far prefer the single hymn of Prudentius, *De Natali Jesu*, to the three little volumes of Accius Syncerus,—so far does this poem fail to suffice for the overthrowing of Goliath as he threatens the church with a sling, or for soothing Saul in his madness with the harp as the preface declares him to do. And I do not know which is more blame-

---

[1] And you therefore the sure hope of gods and men.

worthy for a Christian to handle secular themes in secular language, pretending that he is not a Christian, or in pagan tongue; for the mysteries of Christ ought to be treated in both a scholarly way and reverently. It is not enough to arouse in the reader little temporary feelings of delight; emotions worthy of the Lord must be aroused. And you cannot do this unless you have the subject you are handling thoroughly mastered: for you will not inflame if you yourself are cold; you will not set the reader's mind on fire with the love of celestial things, if you yourself are but lukewarm. If you have at hand either spontaneously or at the cost of no great labor fine phrases and figures to attract the fastidious reader and cause him to linger, I think they ought not to be despised, provided those things which are of chief importance have the first place. Would it be possible for a religious theme to be distasteful to us because it has been clothed in religious language? How can you use religious language if you never take your eyes from Vergil, Horace, and Ovid?—unless, perchance, you approve of those who have described the life of Christ by gathering fragments of Homeric and Vergilian verses from everywhere and sewing them into a patchwork. Surely a painstaking kind of writing,—but have they ever brought tears to the eyes of any? Whom have they moved to pious living? Whom have they recalled from an impure life? And yet not so different is the attempt of those who clothe Christian argument in words, phrases, figures, and rhythms gathered from Cicero. To return, what reward of praise does this rhapsodist gain? This, to be sure, that he has busied himself carefully with Homer and Vergil. What reward of Ciceronianism? That he is applauded only by those who are busied in the same and recognize what has been gathered and whence. This sort of thing certainly furnishes a kind of pleasure, I confess, but to very few and of such a kind that it is easily turned into satiety, and in the end it is nothing more than pleasure. That power of arousing the emotions, without which, in the estimation of Quintilian, there can be no eloquence worthy of admiration, is absolutely lacking. Notwithstanding, we think we are Vergils and Ciceros. Tell me, Nosoponus, if one should break into parts the story of Ganymede elegantly constructed in mosaic and with these same little blocks, by arranging them differently, should attempt to represent Gabriel bearing the divine message to the

Nazarene virgin, would he not produce a rude and disappointing work, out of excellent blocks to be sure, but not fitted to the subject?

No.—Licence granted by the ancients makes excuse for poets.

Bu.—Listen to what Horace says about this:

> [1]*Sed non ut placidis coeant immitia, non ut*
> *Serpentes avibus gcminentur, tigribus agni.*

It is more inappropriate, I think, to join the Muses and Apollo and the rest of the gods of poetry with the mysteries of the Christian religion than to unite snakes with birds and lambs with tigers, especially if in a serious piece of work. And I think that if any thing is sprinkled in by way of a joke from the stories of the ancients, it ought to be endured rather than approved of; for it behooves every speech of Christians to be centered in Christ whereby it will become persuasive, eloquent, and learned. Even boys may practice on serious themes. Who would allow those pagan exercises when practicing for real, serious, and what is still more important, religious subjects?

No.—What then is your advice? That I reject Cicero?

Bu.—No. He should always be in the bosom of the youth who is a candidate for eloquence, but that over-nicety and fastidiousness which causes one to reject a learned and elegant piece of work and to consider it not worth reading simply because it has not been wrought in imitation of Cicero must be absolutely rejected. | In the first place, Ciceronian style does not always accord with one's bent of mind, in which case the effort will turn out badly; in the second place, if one has not the natural ability to attain an inimitable felicity of speaking, what is more stupid than to agonize oneself over the impossible? | Add to this that the Ciceronian style does not fit all subjects nor all characters, and, if it did, it is better sometimes to underdo than to overdo. If his eloquence had cost Cicero as much as it costs the Ciceronians he would have left off some of the ornaments from his orations, I venture to say. That is overdone which is bought at so great a sacrifice of time, health, and even at the price of life itself. That is overdone for the sake of which we neglect the branches

---

[1] But 'twill not screen the unnatural and absurd,
Union of lamb with tiger, snake with bird. Ars Poetica 12, 13.—Conington.

of knowledge more necessary to know. And lastly, that is over-
done which is bought at the expense of piety. If eloquence is
learned to delight the idle, what profits it to learn by heart the
lines of our role by so many vigils? On the contrary, if it
is learned that we may persuade people of those things that are
honorable, Phocion, the Athenian, spoke more effectively than
Demosthenes, Cato of Utica than Cicero. Again, if eloquence is
acquired that our books may wear out with much reading, and if
we could attain without effort the likeness of Ciceronian style,
yet we ought to strive for variety because it would be healing to
the sick stomach of the reader. Variety has such efficacy in human affairs that it is not always expedient to follow even the
best. Ever true is the Grecian proverb, μεταβολὴ πάντων γλυκύ·[1]
Homer and Horace are to be praised for nothing more than
for the fact that their wonderful variety of subject and figure
never allows the reader to grow weary. Besides, | nature has
fashioned us in such way, by granting us each his own genius,
that you will scarcely find two who can do the same thing
or who love the same. | And again, since nothing is more
delicate and fastidious than the human stomach and since
there is such a volume to be devoured by us in order to
gain learning, who could hold out in the continual reading if
all had the same style and diction? Therefore, it is better in
books as it is in banquets that some parts be inferior than that
all be alike. Another illustration : what kind of a host would he be
who would serve many guests of varying taste with the same food
seasoned all alike, even if he were serving Apician delicacies?
The result is now, since one is captivated by one kind of speaking and another by another, that everything is read. Nature too
who intended speech to be a mirror of the mind rebels against
that effort. 'To carry the figure further, | there are as many kinds
of minds as there are forms of voices and the mirror will be
straightway deceptive unless it give back the real image of
the mind, which is the very thing that delights the reader especially—to discover from the language the feelings, the characteristics, the judgment, and the ability of the writer as well as
if one had known him for years. | Out of this has grown the
great variety of preference for books, according as the writer's
genius is kindred or alien, as it wins or repels the reader ; just

---

[1] Change in all things is sweet. Aristotle, Rhet. 1. 11, 20.

as in form and feature different types delight different men. Let
me tell what happened to me. As a youth I was madly in love
with all the poets. But as soon as I became more familiar with
Horace, all others, in comparison to him, began to offend. What
do you think was the reason for this, if not that a kind of secret
affinity of minds was recognized in those mute letters? This
genuine, native quality does not breathe out in the language of
those who express nothing but Cicero. What about the fact that
honorable men though born with only ordinary beauty are never
willing for a portrait to misrepresent them by flattery, and insist
upon being painted in exactly the form that nature has given
them, declaring that it is disgraceful to put a false face upon
any one and that a deceptive mirror or a flattering picture is a
ridiculous thing? The deception would be more disgraceful if
I, Bulephorus, should wish to be thought Nosoponus or any one
else. Are there not some dishonest men who are rightly ridiculed
by the scholars because they reject, as it were, and throw out
of their libraries learned and eloquent authors worthy of immortality, simply because they preferred to express themselves
rather than Cicero, feeling that it would be a kind of imposture
to cast before the eyes of men an illusion of another's beauty
instead of their true selves? I doubt whether, if our Divine
Maker were willing, we could find many who would wish to exchange the whole type of their bodies with others, and still fewer
I suppose there would be who would be inclined to exchange
their minds; because, in the first place, no one would be willing
to be different from what he is and, in the second place, each one
by Providence has been attuned by his own gifts in such a way
that even if he should have some faults he can counterbalance
them by virtues. Each mind has an individuality of its own
reflecting in speech as in a mirror and to fashion it in a different
shape is nothing else than going out in masquerade.

No.—Be careful, lest, as the saying is, your language over-
leap the bounds, for it seems to me that you have reached the
point where you condemn all imitation, overlooking the fact that
the rhetorical schools depend very largely upon rules, imitation,
and practice, unless perchance you believe that those who imitate
Cicero take upon themselves the shape of another while those
who imitate others keep their own.

Bu.—I favor imitation but imitation that aids rather than hinders nature; that corrects rather than destroys nature's gifts. I approve of the imitation of a model agreeing with your genius or at least not antagonistic, for otherwise you would be fighting the battle of the gods and giants. Further, I do not approve of the imitation of one copy from whose lines you would not dare to depart, but that which culls from all authors, and especially the most famous, what in each excels and accords with your own genius,—not just adding to your speech all the beautiful things that you find, but digesting them and making them your own, so that they may seem to have been born from your mind and not borrowed from others, and may breathe forth the vigor and strength of your nature, causing those who read to recognize, instead of a mosaic drawn from Cicero, an offspring of your own brain as they say Minerva was of the brain of Jupiter, reflecting the living image of the parent, so that your speech may not seem a patchwork, but a river flowing forth from the fount of your heart.

But let your first and chief care be to know the subject which you undertake to present. This will furnish you wealth of speech and true, natural emotions. Your language will live, breathe, persuade, convince, and fully express your self.

Nor do I maintain that every thing gained from imitation is spurious. There is some care of the person which is not unbecoming to a man and which sets off native beauty to advantage, —bathing, for example, an office which is of prime importance to good health but which at the same time contributes to beauty of face. Now if you should wish to shape your face after the type of one who is very unlike you, you would accomplish nothing; but if you see that the beauty of some one not so very unlike yourself is lessened by grinning, frowning, wrinkling the forehead, sneering, pouting, winking, and by other like actions, you can, by avoiding these things, make your beauty greater and yet not take on the face of another but mould your own. Likewise if you see that long and shaggy hair is not becoming to another, you may correct yours; if you see that a merry face, a truthful eye, and a countenance so ordered to uprightness that it shows nothing grim or insolent, trivial or unseemly add very much to another's charm, you will be justified in fashioning your face in imitation, since it is natural for the mind to respond to the

face.   Moreover inasmuch as the charm of beauty varies, do
not make up your mind that that beauty is inferior which is
different from the beauty which you admire, for, as we have
said,'those who are most unlike may yet be equal.   And there
is no reason why one very unlike Cicero may not be even
greater than one copying his form more perfectly.   Come then,
let us lay aside our preferences and vote from judgment rather
than feeling.   If your Goddess of Persuasion should give you
the choice of being Quintilian or Cornificius instead of Nosoponus
which would you choose?

No.—For my part, I should prefer to be Quintilian.

Bu.—But yet the other is much more like Cicero.   Which
would you prefer to be, Sallust or Quintus Curtius?

No.—I should prefer Sallust.

Bu.—But Quintus Curtius is more like Cicero.   Would you
prefer to be Leonardo Aretino or Lorenzo Valla?

No.—I should prefer Valla.

Bu.—Yet Leonardo is more like Cicero.   Would you prefer
to be Hermolao Barbaro or Christoforo Landino?

No.—Barbaro.

Bu.—The other is more like Cicero.   Would you prefer to be
Politian or Paolo Cortesi?

No.—Politian.

Bu.—But the other demands that he be called Ciceronian.
Well, would you prefer to be Tertullian, leaving out of consideration his heresy, or Bede?

No.—Tertullian.

Bu.—But Bede has more the phraseology of Cicero.   Would
you prefer to be St. Jerome or Lactantius?

No.—St. Jerome.

Bu.—Yes, but the other, how great an ape of Cicero is he!
You see now that he who is more like Cicero does not necessarily
speak better, and that he who is more unlike does not necessarily
speak worse.   In fine, just as it is possible for many people to
be Atticists and yet be very different, so there is no reason why
many may not be called Ciceronians who are equal though unlike
in power of speaking.   Who can abide those sciolists who reject
with a scowl whatever does not show the lineaments of Ciceronian style which they estimate only by petty words, figures, and
rhythms!   He makes but a feeble effort toward Ciceronian style

who approaches the task without being previously trained by the reading of many authors, by the knowledge of many branches of study, and by acquaintance with a wide range of subjects, not to repeat what has been said about natural ability and practical judgment. I might overlook this foolish little conceit in youth, I might stand it in scholars who counterbalance the fault by many great virtues; but who could endure old men whose only ambition is to be like Cicero, who erase from their list of authors men more learned and more eloquent than themselves because these men dare to vary a little from the lines of Cicero, though they themselves as a rule are so far from being Ciceronians that their speech is even ungrammatical at times? I will not give the names of some I am acquainted with who may perchance hope to become famous thus.

I will speak next of Bartolommeo Scala who thinks Hermolao Barbaro and Politian but indifferent Ciceronians, yet deems himself a true one, however much he tries to conceal it. I, for my part, prefer the dreams of Politian to sober Scala's laborious writings.

Paolo Cortesi acknowledges this ambition but—good heavens! how much farther is his letter from the image of Cicero than the one of Politian which it answers! And in nothing else does Cortesi seem more unlike Cicero than in missing the point in almost the whole argument. He argues the case just as if Politian were keeping him from imitating Cicero and as if he were unwilling that a writer should set before himself a model of any kind; for he reproaches those who, trained by no reading of good authors, no learning, no practice, strive only to gain the form of Cicero and calls them for this reason the apes of Cicero. He reproaches those who borrow words in little bits from Cicero, who walk in others' tracks and create nothing, who do nothing but imitate and imitate only the mere words. He says that he cannot bear those who, though they are anything but Ciceronians, nevertheless laud themselves under the title and do not hesitate to express their opinion of the best writers. Then he advises his friend, after he has by long continued reading dissected, learned by heart, and digested Cicero first and many great writers afterward, to prepare as at any time to write, putting aside that peevish and anxious care to imitate only Cicero, because that anxiety would cause him to attain less

perfectly the very thing he is striving for. Is this keeping one
from imitating Cicero? Does it teach that no one at all is to
be imitated? Does he who is so crammed with reading that the
best from all comes to him for use when writing imitate no one,
even though granting that he is not a slave to any, that he con-
sults his own feelings and takes into consideration the nature
of his subject? Cortesi declares that the apes of Cicero do not
please him, saying: "I wish, my dear Politian, to resemble Cicero
not as an ape resembles a man but as a son resembles his parent,"
making the same remark that Politian had made. Continuing
this speech at length he finally admits, as if forgetting himself,
that he would rather be an ape of Cicero than a son of others.
If this word, *others*, includes Sallust, Livy, Quintilian, Seneca,
who would not prefer to be like them as a son is like a parent
rather than to be like Cicero in the way that an ape is like a
man? Next he makes many charges against those who gorge
themselves with wide reading and do not digest what they read.
Their speech comes out rough, uncouth, and harsh, he says. But
what has this to do with Politian's letter? If he agrees with
him why does he answer as if he disagrees? If he disagrees,
why does he not disprove what Politian says? For it is particularly Ciceronian to discern the subject of dispute, the points
of vantage for the adversary and the main point at issue, and to
say nothing outside the limits of the question. You see then that
Cortesi with much pains worked out an epistle which was more
lengthy than Ciceronian, which elicited no answer from Politian
because of its irrelevancy.

But Politian, who was not styled a Ciceronian, how much
better, albeit in a shorter letter, he expressed Cicero, not only
by the charm of his aphorisms but also by apt, elegant, and
telling language!—though I remember there is a story among
the scholars of Italy that he answered for some reason or other
more curtly than the man deserved. And believe me these things
are not said in disparagement of Cortesi, for it is not a mark
of disrespect for any one to be rated lower than the inimitable
Politian; but they are said to make clear to young men what
it is to be a true Ciceronian.

Hyp.—You lead us by such a round-about way, Bulephorus,
that I am almost Hyponosus instead of Hypologus. Now tell
us simply what you think of Cicero and of imitating him.

No.—This very thing I too should like very much; for your talk has brought me to the point where I have decided to take your advice.

Bu.—I think nothing remains but to summarize what in a scattered fashion has thus far been discussed.

No.—What kind of a man does Cicero seem to you to be?

Bu.—A most excellent orator, and, even though a pagan, a good man, who I think if he had known the Christian religion would have been reckoned among those who now are honored as saints on account of their innocent and pious living. Skill and practice, I confess, aided him very much; but he owed far the greatest part of his eloquence to natural ability, which no one can gain for himself. Nor do I think that any of the other Latin writers ought to be more cherished by boys and young men who are being trained to win praise in the field of eloquence.

Yet I would that the reading of the Latin poets at least came before the study of oratory, for poetry is more in harmony with early youth. Nor would I have any one called to the careful imitation of Cicero until the precepts of the art of rhetoric had been learned. After this I would have a teacher of the art of oratory at hand, just as painters are wont to point out to their pupils when looking at some great picture what has been done in accordance with the principles of art and what in violation of these principles.

I would have Cicero form the first and foremost part of the curriculum but not the only part, and not simply for the purpose of being followed but for being imitated rather and emulated; for he who follows walks in the steps of another and becomes a slave to rules. True indeed is the saying that he cannot walk well who always puts his foot in the track of another, nor swim well who does not dare to throw away the cork. To amplify—an imitator does not desire to say the same things so much as he does to say similar things, nay sometimes not even similar but even equal; an emulator strives even to speak better if he can, and no one was ever so finished an artist that you could not find in his work something which could be done better. But I should not want this imitation to be sought too anxiously and too religiously; for this very thing hinders us from accomplishing our desire.

Nor do I think that Cicero should be adored to the ex-
clusion of all others. You should first read the most noted
authors and cull from them what is best; for it is not necessary that you should imitate any one entirely. Nor do I think
that those ought to be scorned who do not take great delight
in nicety of language but furnish abundance of material for
thought, such as Aristotle, Theophrastus, Pliny. Further I
should not like any one to be so devoted to the imitation of Cicero
that he would depart from the bent of his own genius and follow
at the cost of his health and life what he could never attain because of the limitations of his natural ability; or what, if he
could attain, would be at so great a cost. I should not wish one
to occupy his time exclusively with Cicero, nor do I think that
Ciceronian diction should be aimed at to such a degree that the
liberal arts and especially the necessary ones are neglected. You
must avoid those as you would a pest who cry out that it is
wrong to use any word that is not found in the books of Cicero.
For now that the Latin speech has ceased to be in control, whatever words are discovered in reputable writers, let us use on our
own authority whenever there is need, and if they seem rather
harsh and obsolete, because they are rarely used, let us bring
them forth and by frequent and timely use let us soften them;
for what ground of criticism, pray, can there be if we, aware
that the ancients borrowed words of the Greeks whenever Latin
words were lacking or were considered inadequate, modify what
we find in approved authors when the occasion demands? Not
less zealously ought you to avoid those who declare that whatever
has not been fashioned in imitation of Cicero's words, phrases,
and rhythms must be rejected as entirely unworthy of reading,
notwithstanding it may have other virtues if not similar at least
equal to Cicero's. Let us not have that over fastidious nicety,
or rather let us show seriously in the reading of authors what
Ovid jestingly relates as happening to him in his love affairs:—A
tall girl pleased him because she seemed half divine, a short one
because of her active motion; youth recommended itself to him
through its inherent charm, maturity by its experience of the
world; an ignorant girl delighted him with her simplicity, an
educated one with her intellect; a blond with her wealth of color,
a brunette with some hidden charm or other. If we gather as
freely from the individual writers what they have which is

worthy of approval, we shall spurn none but shall gain something from all to give spice to our speech.

But provision must be made, first of all, that youth, in the simple and untutored time of life, be not deceived by the illusion of a Ciceronian name and become pagan instead of Ciceronian. For we see pests of this kind, not yet absolutely uprooted, from time to time sprouting up again under the guise of old heresies, of Judaism, of paganism. Many years ago, factions of Platonists and Peripatetics began to arise thus among the Italians. Let these names, as sources of discord, be abandoned; let us rather inculcate doctrines which in the pursuit of learning, in religion, and in every phase of life will win and increase our mutual good-will. That belief in sacred things which is truly worthy of a Christian must first be gained. When this is accomplished, nothing will seem more ornamental than the Christian religion, nothing more persuasive than the name of Jesus Christ, nothing more charming than the words by means of which the great men of the Church show forth her mysteries. Nor will the speech of any one seem charming which is not in accord with his character and not accommodated to the subject in hand; that will seem unnatural too which treats of a sacred theme in secular language and which contaminates a Christian theme with pagan baubles. But if some indulgence here is granted to youth, let not more advanced age assume for itself the same right. He who is so much of a Ciceronian that he is not quite a Christian is not even a Ciceronian because he does not speak fittingly, does not know his subject thoroughly, does not feel deeply those things of which he speaks; lastly he does not present his religious beliefs with the same adornment with which Cicero presented the philosophy of his times. The liberal arts, philosophy, and oratory are learned to the end that we may know Christ, that we may celebrate the glory of Christ.

This is the whole scope of learning and eloquence. And we must learn this, viz., that we may imitate what is the essential in Cicero which does not lie in words or in the surface of speech but in facts and ideas, in power of mind and judgment. For what advantage is it if the son reproduce the parent in lines of face when he is unlike him in mind and character? To conclude, if it is not our good fortune to be called Ciceronians by the vote of the ultra Ciceronians we must bear it patiently for the great men whom we have enumerated above suffered the same fate. It is foolish to strive after that which we cannot attain. It is effeminate to torture ourselves pitiably for what so many illustrious writers have borne tranquilly; it is stupid to wish to speak otherwise than the subject demands; it is mad to buy at the price of such vigils what will probably never be of any use. A physician with some such remedy as this cured me, and if you are not too loth to take it, I hope it will cause this fever to leave you, Nosoponus, and you, Hypologus.

Hyp.—I surely have long since been cured of the disease.

No.—And I too, except that I still feel some remnants of that long familiar illness.

Bu.—They will gradually vanish, but if there be any need we will summon again the physician, Reason.

CPSIA information can be obtained
at www.ICGtesting.com
Printed in the USA
BVHW062341160919
558564BV00019B/2361/P